The Observers Series
WILD FLOWERS

About the Book

This book is a pocket guide to the wild flowers most commonly found on country walks, on roadsides and waste land, and even (as 'weeds') in our own gardens. There are full descriptions, each with a detailed colour illustration, of 160 plants; and more than 70 other related species are briefly noted and sometimes also illustrated. The distribution (in western continental Europe as well as in the British Isles) and usual habitats of each species is prominently shown. Plants are grouped according to their families, and family structural characteristics stressed. Basic plant structure is clearly explained in the introduction, and there is a glossary of botanical terms.

About the Author

Francis Rose was, until his retirement in 1981, Reader in Biogeography at King's College, University of London. He is a lifelong botanist whose specialist studies have included the history and distribution of the British and adjacent continental flora: mosses: the effects of air pollution on vegetation: and the ecology and distribution of epiphytic lichens. He is author of many scientific papers, and of several books, including *The Wild Flower Key* and a *Colour Identification Guide to Grasses*.

The Observer's series was launched in 1937 with the publication of *The Observer's Book of Birds*. Today, fifty years later, paperback *Observers* continue to offer practical, useful information on a wide range of subjects, and with every book regularly revised by experts, the facts are right up-to-date. Students, amateur enthusiasts and professional organisations alike will find the latest *Observers* invaluable.

'Thick and glossy, briskly informative' – *The Guardian*

'If you are a serious spotter of any of the things the series deals with the books must be indispensable' – *The Times Educational Supplement*

WILD FLOWERS

Francis Rose,
B.Sc., Ph.D.

Illustrated by R. B. Davis

BLOOMSBURY BOOKS
LONDON

PENGUIN BOOKS

Published by the Penguin Group
Penguin Books Ltd, 27 Wrights Lane, London W8 5TZ, England
Penguin Books USA Inc., 375 Hudson Street, New York, New York 10014, USA
Penguin Books Australia Ltd, Ringwood, Victoria, Australia
Penguin Books Canada Ltd, 2801 John Street, Markham, Ontario, Canada L3R 1B4
Penguin Books (NZ) Ltd, 182–190 Wairau Road, Auckland 10, New Zealand

Penguin Books Ltd, Registered Offices: Harmondsworth, Middlesex, England

First published as *The Observer's Book of Wild Flowers* in small hardback format 1937
Third edition, completely revised and reillustrated 1978
Reprinted 1979, 1981, 1983 (twice), 1988

This edition published by Bloomsbury Books, an imprint of
Godfrey Cave Associates, 42 Bloomsbury Street, London, WC1B 3QJ,
under licence from Penguin Books Limited, 1992

   5 7 9 10 8 6

Printed and bound in Great Britain by
BPCC Hazells Ltd

ISBN 1-8547-1083-4

CONTENTS

PREFACE

In this book 160 plant species are separately illustrated and described. In addition, there are brief descriptive and comparative notes on more than 70 other species that resemble some of them fairly closely. Each reference to one of these additional species, in some cases with an illustration of its key features, is to be found on the page primarily devoted to the description of the plant it most resembles.

It was not very easy to select 160 plants to illustrate. An attempt has been made, however, to include a good range of the most common flowering plants of Great Britain and Ireland, together with some that are locally common in a large part of Britain. In addition, a few others have been included that are not quite so common, but are of special interest for floral, ecological or geographical reasons.

A few of the species included are very rare, or even absent in the British Isles, but very common on the Continent, southwards from Denmark to the River Loire in France; thus this book will serve as a guide to the commoner plants of the lowlands of the whole of north-western Europe.

The descriptions have been made in language as simple and as non-technical as is compatible with clarity and accuracy. Nevertheless, some technical terms have had to be used in order to attain precision, and these terms are explained (with illustrations where necessary) in the glossary.

There is also a list of the plant families represented in this book (showing the abbreviations used for the family names in the individual entries), a list of other abbreviations used in the descriptions, and an index.

All the colour illustrations are by R. B. Davis.

FRANCIS ROSE.

INTRODUCTION

All users of this book, unless already grounded in botanical terminology, are **most strongly advised** to familiarize themselves with the technical terms given in the glossary and to read this introduction, which describes the basic elements of flower structure, **before** consulting any individual entry. Moreover, those using the book in the field are advised to read not only the account of the flower they believe they have found, but also those of other species of the same family, that appear on adjacent pages. This will enable them to check whether or not they have correctly identified the particular plant, and will also rapidly teach them the common features of the main plant families, which are, for reasons of space, not always given in full under every species.

At the beginning of each account there is given in tabulated form the geographical distribution of the species in the British Isles and north-western Continental Europe, a note of its habitats and the normal period of flowering. This information will help the user who believes he or she has found a specific plant to check quickly whether it is, in fact, likely to occur at that particular place and time.

There then follows a detailed description of the plant itself, starting with its habit, root characteristics, leaves and other features, and going on to the form of its inflorescence, continuing with the detailed structure of the flowers and concluding with the form of its fruits. In appropriate cases, closely related or similar plants (other than very rare ones) that might be confused with the illustrated species are then compared with it briefly. In some cases an illustration of the similar plant, or of some distinguishing feature of it, is also given. Flowers and fruits of the main plant are also sometimes separately illustrated, often on a larger scale. Leaves illustrated or outlined separately are usually basal leaves.

It is felt that a short account of the essential features of flower structure will be helpful in this introduction. This section should be read carefully before trying to identify any flower with this book, preferably with an actual flower of some species in hand. For this purpose, it is probably easier to begin with a familiar flower of reasonably large size, as structure is then easier to see. It is unwise to try to begin with a head of small flowers, or a 'double' cultivated flower, as these will cause problems. The study of the structure of smaller flowers, or of heads of aggregated flowers, as in the Daisy family, can be attempted subsequently.

A × 10 hand lens will be found invaluable for studying flower structure, and also such points as the hairs on leaves or the grooves in stems.

The Essential Features of Flower Structure

The first accompanying drawing below illustrates in simple form the structure of an imaginary flower of no particular species, with its parts clearly labelled. Flowers are very varied in form, and it should be remembered that some of the parts shown in the drawing may be missing in some species, or even in some of the flowers of a species; such points are covered in the text where they apply. However, in most cases all the parts illustrated are present, though of varied form; so this illustration serves to show in a general way the relative position and sequence of the parts normally present.

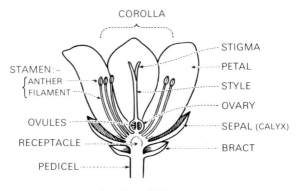

Section of Flower

It is important to remember at the outset that flowers are the sexual reproductive organs of plants, and contain male and female organs; reproduction is the real *raison d'être* of flowers. The amazing variation that exists in flower form and structure is in fact connected with the diverse ways in which evolution has achieved cross-pollination mechanisms, either by various insects, or by the wind.

The flower stalk or *pedicel* normally has at its apex a swelling known as the *receptacle*, to which the parts of the flower are attached.

The outermost whorl of flower parts, known as the *calyx*, is composed of a number of usually leaf-like structures, individually called the *sepals*, whose normal function is to protect the inner parts of the flower in the bud stage. (In some species the calyx is absent, or, as in some members of the Daisy family, represented only by a ring of hairs, the *pappus*, which later becomes a parachute for seed dispersal.)

Within the calyx, the next whorl, the *corolla*, is composed of leaf-like parts, normally coloured, called the *petals*. Their function in most flowers is to make the flower visually attractive to pollinating insects. They may secrete nectar at their bases, or in special spurs, and also may have scent-producing glands, usually at their bases. In wind-pollinated flowers the corolla may be inconspicuous or absent.

Sometimes the sepals are joined together into a *calyx-tube*, and the petals may be joined together into a *corolla-tube*. In such cases the number of the parts can, however, usually be counted from the number of lobes or teeth on the tip of the tube.

The numbers of sepals and petals, and, indeed, of the inner parts, is of great importance in identification; also very significant is the point whether they are free or conjoined. For example, in the Buttercup family (Ranunculaceae) all the parts of the flower are free and separate, while in the Bellflower family (Campanulaceae) the calyx and corolla are both in tubular form; in the Daisy family (Compositae) even the stamens (see below) are joined into a tube. Sometimes the sepals and petals are identical in form and colour; then they are termed collectively a *perianth*, as in the Lily family (Liliaceae).

In some families, eg, those of Dead-Nettles (Labiatae), Peaflowers (Leguminosae) and Orchids (Orchidaceae) the sepals and petals are not in regular symmetrical whorls, but are modified to form flowers of irregular form, symmetrical only about one axis from front to back. Such flowers usually have one, or more, petals enlarged to form a *lip* at the front and a *hood* or arched structure at the back. These flowers are highly adapted to visits by special kinds of insects; the lip forms a landing platform for the insects, while the hood at the rear forms a roof that protects the sexual organs of the flower from rain. The form of such flowers may even be such as to permit only certain kinds of insects to enter. Peaflowers can be seen to have a *keel* of two lower petals in front, partially joined together, two *wings*, one on either side, and a *standard* at the back.

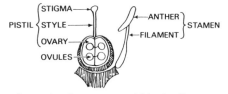

Reproductive organs within the flower

The second drawing illustrates the reproductive organs within the flower. Working from the outside towards the flower's centre, there are first the *stamens*, called collectively the *androecium*. These vary in number, but each stamen consists of a stalk or *filament* and a head or *anther*. The anther contains two or more pollen sacs. The *pollen* consists of microscopic grains – copious and dust-like in wind-pollinated flowers, less plentiful and sticky in insect-pollinated flowers – which contain the male sexual nuclei or *gametes*.

Next there is the female organ of the flower, the *pistil* (or *gynaecium*, as it is now usually called). This comprises a number of parts called *carpels*, which are quite separate in Buttercups but fused together in most families. In a normal fused gynaecium three parts can usually be distinguished. First, at the base, the *ovary*, a little case of one or more *cells*, which contains tiny *ovules*, each holding a single egg. Above the ovary is the stalk-like *style*, which may be single or multiple, and at the tip of each style is a *stigma*, the receptive surface for the pollen.

When pollen is transferred by insects, or wind, to a stigma at the right stage to receive it, each pollen-grain germinates, forming a microscopic tube which grows down inside the style to reach the ovules and their eggs. The male nucleus travels down the tube and fuses with the female nucleus in the egg, and the fertilized egg can then grow into an *embryo*, which, with its coverings, becomes a seed. In time the ovary becomes a seed-box, or fruit.

For purposes of identification the number of carpels is important, and also whether or not they are fused together. In the Buttercup family the carpels are all quite separate, each with its tiny ovary, single short style and stigma on top; in this family they are easy to count, but usually of a large, indefinite number. In most families, where the carpels are fused, their number can be determined either by counting the number of stigmas, or of styles, if these are separate, or else the number of cells in the ovary. The simplest way to see these is to cut (with thumb-nail or penknife) a cross-section of the ovary and examine it with a good hand lens. In some plants, however, it is difficult to count the carpels; in such cases this feature is not used in this book.

Finally, the ovary (in those families where the carpels are fused) may be *superior* or *inferior*. A superior ovary is attached to the receptacle above the corolla-whorl; an inferior ovary has the calyx and the corolla arising from its top, so that it can be seen below the flower in side view. This character is important, for example, in distinguishing the Campanulaceae, with inferior ovaries, from the Gentianaceae (Gentian family), with superior ovaries. Similarly, the Liliaceae have superior ovaries, and the Iridaceae (Iris family), inferior ones.

The families are arranged in this book in the accepted scientific order of J. Dandy's *List of British Vascular Plants*. In general the earlier families have free, regular parts and superior ovaries; families next described have the corollas in the form of tubes; later still in the list are irregular two-lipped flowers; then flowers with inferior ovaries; finally, among the Dicotyledons, the Compositae, with tiny flowers with tubular corollas and inferior ovaries massed into heads. The last part of the book covers the Monocotyledons which usually have their flower parts in threes, rather than in fives or fours as in the Dicotyledons, and usually have parallel-veined leaves.

Many other points about flower and fruit structure are discussed in the text, and the technical terms used are defined in the glossary.

Inflorescences. Flowers may be borne singly, that is, they are *solitary*, as in the Primrose and Daffodil, or they may be grouped together in various ways into an *inflorescence*. If the inflorescence (or single flower stalk) is devoid of leaves from the base, it is called a *scape*. The various forms of inflorescence mentioned in the text (*cyme, raceme, spike, umbel, panicle, corymb*) are defined in the glossary, as are the leaves found in an inflorescence (*bracts* and *bracteoles*). A final word may, however, be said about the peculiar inflorescences of the Compositae and the Dipsaceae (Teasel family), in which the flowers are grouped into a head (*capitulum*) of unstalked tiny *florets* on a common receptacle. The whole may be mistaken for a single flower, especially if, as in the Daisy, there are symmetrical *ray-florets* at its outer edge which look like petals. Examination with a lens will, however, show the structure of the numerous tiny florets, each with a corolla and tube of stamens, with a corolla and a style, or with both stamens and style.

Note. The scientific names of the plants mentioned follow *Flora Europaea*, by T. G. Tutin and others, Cambridge University Press, 5 volumes, 1964–80. The English names, with a few exceptions, follow The Botanical Society of the British Isles' *English Names of Wild Flowers*, Butterworths, 1974.

GLOSSARY

Achene A dry, non-splitting one-seeded fruit.

Annual Plants flowering and fruiting in the same year as the seeds germinate, and then dying.

Arrow-shaped leaf A wide-based leaf, tapering to a point above, with two downward-directed pointed basal lobes.

Awl-shaped leaf One tapering from a cylindrical base to a fine point.

Axil The angle between a leaf or its stalk and the stem.

Berry A soft, fleshy fruit containing seeds without a stony wall around each.

Biennial Plants flowering and fruiting in the year following that in which the seeds germinate, and then dying.

Bract A modified leaf with a flower, or inflorescence, in its axil.

Bracteole A small bract on the stalk of a flower, without a flower in its own axil.

Calyx The whorl of sepals in a flower.

Capitulum The dense head of inflorescence of stalkless small flowers found in Compositae and Dipsaceae.

Capsule A dry fruit that splits open to release the seeds by valves (qv).

Carpel One of the divisions of the ovary or seed-vessel.

Clasping leaf A stalkless leaf with basal lobes, called *auricles*, that partly enclose the stem.

Arrow-shaped leaf

Bract

Compound leaf A leaf divided into separate leaflets.

Corolla The whorl of petals in a flower.

Corymb A cyme (qv) in which the flowers are all more or less at the same level in a flat-topped cluster.

Cyme An inflorescence that terminates in a flower that opens first, with side branches that terminate in like manner. The branches may be always to one side at a time; or in opposite pairs, as in the drawing; this second type is typical of the Caryophyllaceae.

Digitate leaf A compound leaf divided into leaflets radiating like the fingers of a spread hand.

Dimorphic Flowers that appear in two forms in the same species, on the same or different plants.

Dioecious plants Those plants with male and female flowers on separate individual plants.

Drupe A fleshy fruit in which the seeds inside are enclosed in hard stony walls, as in a cherry or plum.

Elliptical Of a narrow oval shape, tapering at both ends.

Entire leaf A leaf without lobes or teeth.

Epicalyx A whorl of bracteoles (qv) outside the calyx, resembling an extra calyx.

Family A natural grouping of genera, which have important structural characters of the flowers in common.

Filament The stalk of a stamen.

Follicle A dry capsular fruit splitting down one side, containing several seeds, and derived from a single carpel.

Genus (plural, *genera*) A group of species that have characters in common and are closely related.

Heart-shaped leaf Broad below, pointed above, with two rounded basal lobes.

Herb A plant that dies back to the ground in autumn and is not woody.

Inferior ovary An ovary developed below the calyx and corolla, with the rest of the flower sitting on top of it.

Inflorescence The grouping of flowers on a plant.

Involucre A series of bract-like leaves below an inflorescence or flower-head.

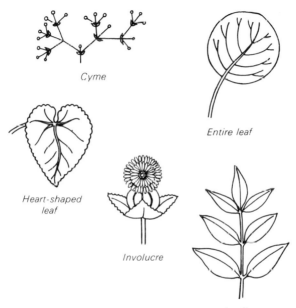

Cyme

Entire leaf

Heart-shaped
leaf

Involucre

Leaflets

Keel The two lower front petals in a Peaflower, forming a boat-shaped structure.

Kidney-shaped leaf A leaf of rounded outline with the stalk in a notch between two rounded basal lobes.

Lance-shaped leaf A long narrow leaf, wider below, gradually tapered to a point at the tip.

Latex A milky juice found in certain plants.

Leaflets The separate parts of a compound leaf.

Linear leaf A long, very narrow leaf with more or less parallel sides, as in grasses and daffodils.

Node A point on the stem at which leaves or branches arise, sometimes swollen.

Oblong leaf   *Oval leaves*

Oblong leaf   A leaf about twice or three times as long as broad, with rounded ends, and parallel-sided in the middle part.

Oval leaf   Shaped like an egg in outline – broader than an elliptical leaf.

Palmate leaf   A leaf lobed like the palm of a hand with veins radiating from the stalk.

Panicle   An inflorescence that is a branched raceme (qv).

Pappus   A parachute mechanism for seed dispersal, formed from hairs. In the Daisy family these replace the calyx.

Pedicel   The stalk of a single flower.

Peduncle   The common stalk of several flowers, or of an inflorescence.

Perennial   Plants that live for more than two years.

Perianth   A term used to cover both calyx and corolla, especially when they are indistinguishable in form and colour.

Perfoliate leaf   A stalkless single leaf which forms a ring round a stem, so that the stem passes through it.

Panicle   *Perfoliate leaf*

Petiole   The stalk of a leaf.

Pinnate leaf   A compound leaf with the leaflets arranged along either side of a common stalk, usually in opposite pairs.

Pinnatifid leaf   A leaf that is deeply cut into lobes along either side of the midrib, but *not* so far that separate leaflets are formed.

Raceme   An inflorescence of elongated shape with flowers along a stem in which the lowest flower opens first, and then the others in sequence upward.

Radical or root-leaves   Leaves that arise directly from the root-stock or the base of the stem.

Scape   A leafless flower-stalk, bearing one or more flowers, that arises directly from the root-stock or stem-base.

Sepal   One of the outer floral leaves that together comprise the calyx.

Sessile   Stalkless leaves or flowers, arising directly from the stem.

Simple leaf   A leaf not divided into separate leaflets; it may, however, be lobed or toothed.

Spadix   An inflorescence of sessile flowers arranged around a thick fleshy stem, usually within a spathe.

Spathe   A large bract (or pair of bracts) that envelops certain types of inflorescence, especially in bud.

Species   A population of plant individuals, all of which resemble one another closely in all important structural characters, and are normally capable of cross-breeding within the population, though not necessarily outside it.

Raceme   *Simple leaf*

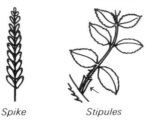

Trifoliate leaf

Spike   *Stipules*

Spike A raceme in which the flowers are sessile, that is, have no foot stalks or pedicels.

Spoon-shaped leaf A blunt leaf, widest near the tip, and tapering quickly to the base or into the stalk.

Spreading Used of petals or sepals, those that stand out at right angles to the axis of the flower; used of hairs, those similarly angled to the surface from which they arise.

Standard The petal at the back of a Peaflower.

Stipules Small leaf-like structures, normally in pairs, at the point where a leaf-stalk joins the stem.

Stolon A runner above ground.

Superior ovary An ovary developed above, and free from, the whorls of petals and sepals.

Terminal At the end of a stem or branch.

Trifoliate leaf A compound leaf with three leaflets only.

Tubercle A small swelling or knob.

Umbel A more or less flat-topped inflorescence, with the outer flowers opening first, in which the foot-stalks of the flowers radiate like the ribs of an umbrella. In *compound umbels*, the branches bear umbels in their turn.

Valve A flap or tooth by which a capsule opens to release its seeds.

Wing One of the side petals in a Peaflower.

Compound umbel

ABBREVIATIONS OF FAMILY NAMES

ADO	Adoxaceae	*Moschatel family*
AMA	Amaryllidaceae	*Daffodil family*
AQU	Aquifoliaceae	*Holly family*
ARA	Araliaceae	*Ivy family*
ARC	Araceae	*Arum family*
BOR	Boraginaceae	*Borage family*
CAM	Campanulaceae	*Bellflower family*
CAR	Caryophyllaceae	*Pink family*
CHE	Chenopodiaceae	*Goosefoot family*
CIS	Cistaceae	*Rockrose family*
COM	Compositae	*Daisy family*
CON	Convolvulaceae	*Bindweed family*
CRU	Cruciferae	*Cabbage family*
CUC	Cucurbitaceae	*Gourd family*
DIP	Dipsacaceae	*Teasel family*
DRO	Droseraceae	*Sundew family*
EMP	Empetraceae	*Crowberry family*
ERI	Ericaceae	*Heath family*
EUP	Euphorbiaceae	*Spurge family*
FUM	Fumariaceae	*Fumitory family*
GEN	Gentianaceae	*Gentian family*
GER	Geraniaceae	*Crane's-bill family*
GUT	Guttiferae	*St John's-wort family*
IRI	Iridaceae	*Iris family*
LAB	Labiatae	*Deadnettle family*
LEG	Leguminosae	*Pea family*
LIL	Liliaceae	*Lily family*
LOR	Loranthaceae	*Mistletoe family*
LYT	Lythraceae	*Loosestrife family*
MAL	Malvaceae	*Mallow family*
MEN	Menyanthaceae	*Bogbean family*
NYM	Nymphaeaceae	*Water-lily family*
ONA	Onagraceae	*Willowherb family*
ORC	Orchidaceae	*Orchid family*
OXA	Oxalidaceae	*Wood-sorrel family*
PAP	Papaveraceae	*Poppy family*
PLA	Plantaginaceae	*Plantain family*
PLU	Plumbaginaceae	*Sea Lavender family*
PGA	Polygalaceae	*Milkwort family*
PGO	Polygonaceae	*Dock family*
PRI	Primulaceae	*Primrose family*
RAN	Ranunculaceae	*Buttercup family*

RES	Resedaceae	*Mignonette family*
ROS	Rosaceae	*Rose family*
RUB	Rubiaceae	*Bedstraw family*
SAX	Saxifragaceae	*Saxifrage family*
SCR	Scrophulariaceae	*Figwort family*
SOL	Solanaceae	*Nightshade family*
TYP	Typhaceae	*Reed-mace family*
UMB	Umbelliferae	*Parsley or Carrot family*
URT	Urticaceae	*Nettle family*
VIO	Violaceae	*Violet family*

GENERAL ABBREVIATIONS

ab	abundant	**hbs**	hedgebanks
an	annual	**hs**	hedges
ar	arable	**hths**	heaths
bi	biennial	**mds**	meadows
c	common	**mls**	moorlands
chk	chalk	**mts**	mountains
decid	deciduous	**o**	occasional
dist	distribution	**per**	perennial
f	frequent	**r**	rare
fc	fairly common	**rds**	roadsides
fam	family	**ssp**	subspecies
fl	flowering time	**v**	very
gdns	gardens	**wa**	wastelands
gslds	grasslands	**wds**	woodlands
hab	habitat		

Countries of Distribution

BR ISLES	British Isles	**IRE**	Ireland
ENG	England	**SCOT**	Scotland
GB	Great Britain	**EUR**	Continental Western Europe

Months (of flowering) are given in numeral form (eg March = 3).

Scale drawings: ×2 = twice actual size
×1 = life size
×0·5 = half actual size

Fam: RAN.   *Dist:* Br Isles and W Eur.
Hab: Damp situations; conspicuous in riverside mds, fens, wet alder and willow wds, and on upland lake shores. Fl 3–5.

Rootstock thick, producing stout hollow stems that bear broadly heart-shaped glossy green leaves, 4–8 cm across, with v large stipules at their bases. After flowering, the root-leaves persist and become much larger. Flowers have no true petals – instead, there are five broad glossy yellow petal-like sepals and many golden stamens. In the centre there are several carpels which develop on fertilization into green sac-like follicles up to 1 cm long, each with several seeds inside (not into tiny, one-seeded achenes as in Buttercups). All the Ranunculaceae are poisonous and are normally avoided by grazing animals.

WOOD ANEMONE

Anemone nemorosa

Fam: RAN.   *Dist:* GB and most of W Eur.
Hab: ab in decid wds; also in old hbs and upland mds.
Fl 3–4.

Per herb, with fleshy creeping underground rhizome, which
puts up stems, each bearing a simple white star-like flower.
Halfway up the stem, a whorl of three green palmate leaves
with toothed segments. Long-stalked leaves also arise separately, from the rhizome, a little later. Each flower has
normally six petal-like segments in a single whorl. Flowers
sometimes pink-tinged inside, and normally purple-flushed
outside, especially on the drooping buds. Many stamens;
numerous separate carpels, each with a short-pointed style,
developing into achenes similar to those of Buttercups. By
mid June the plant is hard to find except in more northern
districts; it soon dies down. Of great beauty and delicacy, it
would be much sought after if it were rare.

Fam: RAN.   *Dist:* S Eng, Wales, W Eur. Not native N of a line from Morecambe Bay to Sheffield, nor in Denmark. *Hab:* c in chalk and limestone districts. Fl 7–8.

This climbing shrub, clinging to other shrubs, trees and hedges, is one of the few woody climbers (*lianes*) in Br flora. Its pinnately compound leaves have stalks which can curl tightly like tendrils round any support. The leaflets, in opposite pairs, bear a few large blunt teeth. Flowers, fragrant, have only one floral whorl of four cream-coloured segments, downy outside. Many stamens, massed around the central cluster of long hairy styles; these elongate in fruit to form a feathery plume on each of the numerous achenes. The plumes act as a means of wind-dispersal for the fruits. In autumn the plant, from its masses of plumed fruits, may give the appearance of wreaths of smoke or hair on wood borders or hedges, hence its other name of Old Man's Beard.

BULBOUS BUTTERCUP   *Ranunculus bulbosus*

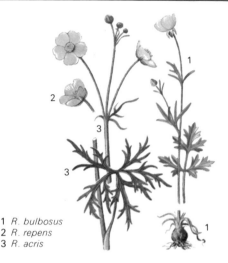

1 *R. bulbosus*
2 *R. repens*
3 *R. acris*

Fam: RAN.   *Dist:* Br Isles and W Eur.
Hab: c in drier pastures, now most c on the older gslds of
chalk and limestone hills. Fl 5–6.

There are three widespread and c species of Buttercup. All
have flowers with five shiny yellow petals and five green
sepals; many yellow stamens and a central group of
numerous green carpels, each distinct and ripening into a
head of tiny brown achenes. Leaves are compound and
hairy; the petals have nectar-producing scales at their base.
R. bulbosus has a corm-like swelling at the base of the erect
stem, three-lobed root-leaves and a furrowed pedicel, with
bent back (reflexed) sepals.

Meadow Buttercup, *R. acris*, is a plant of damper mds with
no basal corm; unfurrowed flower-stalk, spreading sepals.
Creeping Buttercup, *R. repens*, grows in damp wds and on
waste; creeping stems, furrowed flower-stalks and spreading
sepals to its deeper yellow flowers.

24

COMMON WATER-CROWFOOT

Ranunculus aquatilis

Fam: RAN. *Dist:* Br Isles and W Eur.
Hab: c in ponds, ditches, unless too polluted Fl 5–6.

The Water-crowfoots have the flower structure of Buttercups, so they are included in that genus, but they always have white, not yellow flowers, and are more or less aquatic in habit. There are several species of Water-crowfoot, too much alike for the beginner to distinguish. The species illustrated, *R. peltatus*, has both rounded floating leaves on long stalks, and submerged leaves much divided into fairly stiff, hair-like green segments. Flowers are up to about 2 cm across, with five petals, and five green sepals below; there is a yellow spot at the base of each petal.

The other Water-crowfoots differ in whether they have both floating and submerged leaves, in size of flowers and shape of leaves, and in the hairiness or otherwise of the carpels. Some, such as River Water-crowfoot, *R. fluitans*, are confined to fast-running water and may lack floating leaves; others, such as Ivy-leaved Water-crowfoot, *R. hederaceus*, have only the rounded type of leaf and they are usually found on muddy ground, not in water.

Fam: RAN. *Dist:* Br Isles and W Eur.
Hab: hbs and most wds on less acid soils. Fl 2–5.

A little plant, with burnished gold, star-like flowers. The
root-leaves are heart-shaped, long-stalked, glossy dark
green, and hairless; the stem-leaves are smaller and more
toothed. The flowers have usually three yellow-green sepals,
seven-twelve (usually eight) glossy yellow petals, narrower
than in other Buttercups, and many stamens and carpels.
The roots produce cylindrical fleshy tubers. Tiny bulbils,
found in the leaf-axils of one variety of this plant, form a
means of vegetative reproduction. This species has normally
dried up and disappeared by mid-May. It is normally of
tufted growth but may produce runners which can root and
form new plants. A Buttercup, it is not related to the Greater
Celandine, which is of the Poppy family (Papaveraceae).

1 *N. lutea* and leaf
2 *N. alba* and leaves

Fam: NYM.   *Dist:* Br Isles and W Eur.
Hab: ponds, canals, slow-flowing rivers. Fl 6–8.

Rootstock massive and fleshy, creeping in the mud below water. It bears leathery, light-green heart-shaped floating leaves on v long, elastic stalks. The leaves' upper surface bears a waxy cuticle, pierced by minute stomata which exchange oxygen and carbon dioxide with the atmosphere, as do the leaves of land plants; their lower surface, of spongy tissue with no cuticle, is typical of lower leaves of aquatic plants. Submerged leaves' are of flaccid, wholly spongy texture. Air-canals traversing leaves and stalks give buoyancy, and conduct oxygen to the submerged parts. Flowers have five or six large yellow broad concave sepals, and about 20 less conspicuous narrower yellow petals, which secrete nectar at their bases. Stamens large and v numerous. The many-celled ovary is flask-shaped, with a 'lid' marked with radiating stigmas. When over-ripe it smells of alcohol, hence the old name of 'Brandy-bottle'.

White Water-lily, *Nymphaea alba*, more local as a native plant, has much larger, usually white flowers (pink forms are cultivars); four green sepals; 20–25 long white petals; leaves almost circular.

COMMON POPPY   *Papaver rhoeas*

Fam: PAP.   *Dist:* Br Isles and W Eur.
Hab: formerly ab in cornfields; now much reduced by
herbicides, but still f on disturbed ground and rds on sandy
or chalky soils. Fl 6–9.

Branched bristly stems bear roughly hairy pinnate leaves.
Magnificent scarlet flowers, up to 8 cm across. The two
green bristly concave sepals fall off as the flowers expand, to
reveal the four rather crumpled petals. Numerous, bluish-
black stamens surround the globular ovary, which bears a
disc of 8–12 radiating lobes representing the stigmas. The
ripe seed capsule, globose and hairless, releases its seeds
through pores below the stigma disc.
    Other rarer poppies differ in ripe fruits, smooth-oblong in
P. dubium, bristly-oblong in *P. argemone*, bristly-globose in *P.
hybridum*. All poppies contain an acrid narcotic latex in
canals in their stems.

Fam: PAP.   *Dist.* W Eur and Br Isles except N Scot.
Hab: coasts, on shingly seashores above high-tide level.
Fl 6–9.

Horned-poppy is closely related to the true Poppies, but
differs in its fruits. A bi or per plant, it has a basal rosette of
fleshy bluish-grey, bristly pinnatifid leaves 10–15 cm long,
from which arise spreading branched stems 30–90 cm tall,
bearing similar but clasping, less divided leaves, and striking
clear yellow four-petalled flowers 6–9 cm across. As in true
Poppies, the two concave sepals that protect the crumpled
bud fall off when it opens. Numerous yellow stamens; a long
narrow ovary divided into two cells with a bilobed stigma on
top. In fruit the ovary develops into a rough but hairless
narrow sickle-shaped pod, 15–30 cm long. The plant is still c
where seaside visitors have not trampled it to death.

Fam: PAP.   *Dist:* Br Isles and W Eur.
Hab: hbs and wa near houses. Fl 5–8.

This plant, related to the Poppies (and not to Lesser Celandine, which is a Buttercup), is a per with erect branched stems 30–90 cm tall, bearing rather thin leaves with toothed leaflets, yellow-green above, grey-green below. Flowers, 2–2·5 cm across, are borne in loose umbels on long stalks, and have two greenish-yellow hairy sepals, four clear yellow petals, and numerous stamens. The fruit, 3–5 cm long, is elongated, and divides into two valves that open from below upwards. The bright orange latex in the canals of stem and leaves is acrid and poisonous, and was once used for destroying warts. The plant is not found in natural vegetation in W Eur and is probably an old introduction for medicinal purposes.

Fam: FUM.   *Dist:* Br Isles (most c in S and E), and W Eur.
Hab: cornfields, open wa, especially on chalky soil. Fl 5–9.

This elegant little an plant has delicate-looking leaves, of a
glaucous grey-green colour, much divided into thin flat
narrow segments. Its stems, 10–30 cm tall, bear leaf-opposed
racemes of 10–40 small flowers, each of which has a narrow
bract. Each flower has two pink heart-shaped sepals, and
four long narrow pink petals tipped with dark red. The
upper petal is spurred below, and the two lateral ones are
joined at their tips to enclose the two branched stamens and
the pistil in a tubular corolla. The ovary consists of a single
carpel which ripens to a small compressed globular nut 2–
2·5 cm wide.

    There are several other species distinguished by leaf
shape, flower colour and shape, and size and shape of fruits.

Fam: CRU.   *Dist:* Br Isles and W Eur.
Hab: quite c locally in cornfields, especially on chalky or sandy soils, though modern agricultural herbicides have reduced it to some extent. Fl 5–8.

A roughly hairy an, its stalked lyre-shaped lower leaves are bristly and strongly toothed; the sessile upper ones are simple. The strong stem, 30–60 cm tall, bears terminal racemes of four-petalled yellow flowers 10–15 mm across. The pods are hairy, with a straight conical beak above, more than half as long as the two valves, which are strongly veined, and have 6–12 red-brown seeds in each cell.

White Mustard, *S. alba*, is a similar-looking plant often confused with Charlock, but if found wild is an escape from cultivation. It has a strongly-compressed, almost winged, sabre-like beak to its fruit, which is as long as the valves or longer, and all the leaves are pinnately lobed.

SHEPHERD'S-PURSE   *Capsella bursa-pastoris*

Fam: CRU.   *Dist.* Br Isles and most of Eur.
Hab: ar, gardens, waysides, wa. Fl all year.

Its deep taproot supports a rosette of normally deeply and
sharply pinnately-lobed radical leaves. Stem-leaves are
arrow-shaped and clasping, usually toothed. The tiny
flowers, 2·5–3·0 mm across, with four green sepals and four
white petals twice their length, are borne in terminal
racemes on the stems. Fruits are heart-shaped on long stalks,
and when ripe split into two valves, releasing the many tiny
seeds. Currently one of the world's most successful plants, it
tends to form distinctive local populations, probably because it can pollinate itself, and withstands both droughts
and cold weather.

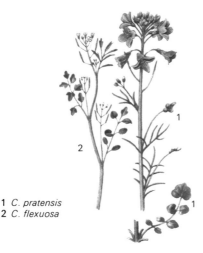

1 *C. pratensis*
2 *C. flexuosa*

Fam: CRU.   *Dist.* Br Isles and W Eur.
Hab: Damp wds, swamps, marshy mds. Fl 3–6.

Attractive per herb with flowers rosy-pink fading to whitish. Stems erect, 20–40 cm tall, have pinnate root-leaves with rounded leaflets; leaflets of stem-leaves are much narrower. Raceme, bearing four-petalled flowers of typical Crucifer form, 1·0–1·8 cm across, is first dome-shaped, later elongated as the fruits develop below. Four sepals, six yellow stamens, two stigmas. Seed-pod upright, v slender, 25–40 mm long. The ripe pod bursts into two valves, ejecting seeds up to 2 m away. Runners are often produced from the rootstock. Sometimes called Milkmaids or Lady's-smock.

Wavy Bitter-cress, *C. flexuosa*, of similar dist and hab, has much smaller flowers with narrow white petals less than 5 mm long and scarcely longer than the sepals. No runners; hairy wavy stem; egg-shaped to elliptical terminal leaflets to its leaves.

1 flower
2 fruit

Fam: CRU.   *Dist:* c in lowlands of Br Isles, W Eur.
Hab: moving water, especially calcareous. Fl 5–10.

This per herb, 20–60 cm high, has hollow succulent stems
which bear glossy dark green pinnate leaves. The terminal
leaflet of each leaf is roundish to heart-shaped, the pairs of
lateral leaflets egg-shaped or elliptical and only feebly
toothed (never with sharp teeth as in Fool's Water-cress,
Apium nodiflorum, sometimes eaten in mistake for it). The
small white flowers, borne in racemes at the tips of the stems,
are typical of the Crucifer family, with four short green
sepals, four longer white petals 2–3 mm long, six stamens,
and an ovary of two fused carpels with two short styles. After
fertilization the racemes lengthen and the ovaries develop
into two-valved seed-pods, 13–18 mm long. This plant, with
bred varieties and hybrids, forms the familiar salad plant,
remaining green all year. It should be carefully washed
before being eaten, because of the risk of parasites on it
entering the human body.

GARLIC MUSTARD *Alliaria petiolata*

Fam: CRU.   *Dist:* Br Isles north to Ross-shire; W Eur.
Hab: c on hbs, shady banks, beechwoods on chalky soils.
Fl 4–6.

Bi herb, also known as Jack-by-the-hedge, is easily recognized by the strong smell of garlic produced on bruising the leaves or stems. It has an erect little branched stem, 20–100 cm tall, with long-stalked kidney-to-heart-shaped root-leaves 6–10 cm across that are shiny above and hairy below. Stem-leaves are short-stalked, smaller and more toothed. The flowers, borne in long racemes on the tips of the stems, are about 6 mm across, white and four-petalled. The seed-pods are 35–60 mm long, with two keeled valves so as to be four-angled, and curve at the base so as to stand vertically on their rather thick spreading stalks. The Orange-tip Butterfly caterpillar feeds on the pods, but it is difficult to see because pods and caterpillar are so alike. The big root-leaves are conspicuous throughout the winter.

WILD MIGNONETTE   *Reseda lutea*

Fam: RES.   *Dist:* c in S half Eng; W Eur: f in Ire.
Hab: rds, ar, disturbed wa; chalky soils. Fl 6–8.

Bi to per plant resembling garden Mignonette but scentless,
with smaller flowers. Leaves deeply pinnatifid in blunt,
wavy narrow lobes. Flowers in long terminal racemes; six
narrow unequal sepals. Usually six greenish-yellow petals;
upper two three-lobed, lateral pair two-three-lobed, the two
lower narrow and undivided. Many stamens on a disc that
secretes nectar. Ovary of three diverging short carpels opens
for pollination, with three stigmas outspread. Seed capsule,
12–18 mm long, stout, three-lobed, wrinkled; several black
shiny seeds in each cell.

  Weld, *R. luteola*, bi of similar dist and hab, taller, more
erect. Inflorescences longer; four sepals, four petals;
numerous strap-shaped, shiny, wrinkled, un-divided, untoothed leaves, many in basal rosette.

1 *V. hirta*
2 *V. odorata*

Fam: VIO.   *Dist:* c in S half Eng, NW Eur; r and eastern in Scot; very r Ire.
Hab: Dry chalk and limestone gslds. Fl 3–early 5.

The thick, rather woody rootstock produces tufts of narrowly heart-shaped leaves; these, with their 2–4 cm-long stalks, are densely hairy. Flowers scentless, pale blue-violet, on longer stalks, have five small green appendaged sepals and five blunt petals, the lowest of which forms a lip with a pale spot at the base and a pale blue spur. Five short orange stamens, fairly conspicuous. There is a single style and the ripe capsule is egg-shaped and downy. This plant beautifies the chalk downlands at a season when little else is in flower.

Sweet Violet, *V. odorata*, is similar-looking, with usually larger flowers that are either deep violet-coloured or white and with the well-known violet odour. Its leaves are much broader than those of Hairy Violet, sometimes almost kidney-shaped, dark glossy green and much less hairy, except sometimes on the stalks. It is a plant of hbs, lanesides and wd borders, mainly on calcareous soils, and is still not uncommon southwards from central Scot and in Ire and W Eur. It is certainly a native, but often a garden escape.

COMMON DOG VIOLET   *Viola riviniana*

Fam: VIO.   *Dist:* Br Isles and W Eur.
Hab: c in wds, mds, hbs, mt rocks. All soils except acid or v wet. Fl 3–5. Inconspicuous, self-pollinating flowers with tiny green petals, or none, may fl 7–9.

The most c Violet, its per erect rootstock produces flowering stems around a central, non-flowering rosette of leaves. Leaves heart-shaped, usually hairless, 2–3 cm long, borne on stalks two or three times their length. Where these join stem, there are lance-shaped stipules fringed with long narrow appendages. Flowers, borne singly, on stalks 5–7 cm long and in the leaf-axils, are scentless, each with five petals, the lowest larger and longer, forming a lip. This has a pale base inside, marked with long, radiating purple veins; on its back an even paler hollow, blunt, curved spur, notched at the tip. Five small stamens; one style. The ripe capsule, ovoid but three-sided, opens into three valves to release seeds.

Early Dog-violet, *V. reichenbachiana.* Similar, r in Scot; hab wds on calcareous soils. Flowers paler, more lilac, with dark, straight, more conical spur to the lip, and tiny sepal appendages.

COMMON MILKWORT   *Polygala vulgaris*

Fam: PGA.   *Dist:* Br Isles and W Eur.
Hab: locally c in old dry gslds and fixed sand-dunes, especially on calcareous soils. Fl 5–9.

A low-growing per herb with a woody base-stem which forms loose mats of shoots bearing lance-shaped alternately-placed, acute leaves, 5–30 mm long. Upper leaves longer than lower. Flowers in loose racemes, purplish-or slaty-blue, purple, pink, white, mauve. Each flower has two large, 5–6 mm-long, lateral coloured sepals, and three much smaller greenish outer ones. Petals whitish, enclosed by the lateral sepals, fringed and conjoined. Eight stamens are joined into a tube. In fruit the lateral sepals turn green except for their darker veins, and are adpressed to the flattened egg-shaped two-celled capsule.

Heath Milkwort, *P. serpyllifolia*, is more c than *P. vulgaris* in W and N Br and on acid gslds and heaths. Its leaves are in opposite pairs, its flower tints darker; growth is slenderer, more sprawling. Chalk Milkwort, *P. calcarea*, only on chalk gslds in S Eng, has basal rosettes of leaves; all leaves blunt and broadest near top; flowers gentian blue (or pink or white); sepals blunt.

Fam: GUT.   *Dist.* Bᵣ Isles except N Scot; W Eur.
Hab: c in rds, hbs, downs, scrub; less acid, dry soils. Fl 6–9.

Per herb with creeping rootstocks. Erect hairless two-edged stems bear pairs of oblong-to-elliptic stalkless opposite leaves, 1–2 cm long, with many translucent veins and dots, that contain a clear oily liquid. Flowers yellow, in opposite-branched cymes. Five narrow pointed green sepals; five longer golden-yellow spreading petals about 1 cm long. Sepals and petal-edges bear black dot-like glands. Numerous golden stamens, gathered into three bundles. Three long styles above ovary, which after fertilization forms a pear-shaped capsule opening by three slits.

Hairy St John's-wort, *H. hirsutum*, of similar looks and dist, but more confined to basic or to clayey soils: leaves downy and 2–5 cm long, without pellucid dots or veins; pale yellow flowers, and many black stalked glands on the sepals. Many other species.

COMMON ROCK-ROSE

Helianthemum nummularium

1 back of flower, showing sepals

Fam: CIS. *Dist:* W Eur and GB (except Cornwall, NW Scot, some islands); one spot in Donegal, Ire.
Hab: f and ab on gslds, banks, on calcareous soil; in Scot on rd banks among Heather. Fl 5–9.

This delightful plant is a dwarf, creeping shrub, 30 cm high or, usually, much less. Leaves narrow, oblong, about 0·5–2·5 cm long, green above and white-woolly beneath, untoothed. Pairs of narrow stipules at leaf-bases are longer than the short leaf-stalks. Flowers are in lax inflorescences of 1–12, with woolly stalks; each has three large downy sepals with strong green veins, and two tiny scale-like sepals that are easily overlooked. Five yellow petals, crinkly like those of Poppies as the flower opens and smoother later; normally lasting only one day. Many golden stamens surround the globular ovary, which has a cap-like stigma and develops into a three-valved capsule.

Fam: CAR.   *Dist:* W Eur, Br Isles; r in NW Scot, N Ire.
Hab: rds, downs, wa, c clk and light soils. Fl 6–9.

Per plant, 30–60 cm tall. Stems usually hairy, erect, bear
pairs of opposite branches in axils of pointed elliptic, grey-
green, hairless leaves. Inflorescence has *dichasium*, form
characteristic of the CAR, in which axis repeatedly branches
into threes, each central stem bearing a single flower, lateral
stems branching again into three. Sepals joined into five-
toothed tubular bladder-like (hence the English name)
glaucous grey-green calyx, with a network of darker purplish nerves. Five petals, separate, white, each cloven into
two narrow segments, and bearing a pair of white scales on
the upper side, below the cleft. Petals' long fine stalks are
hidden within the calyx. Ten stamens; one-celled ovary
bearing three stigmas at apex. Fruit is a capsule with six
teeth at apex.

Sea Campion, *S. vulgaris* ssp *maritima*, c on seashores, cliffs,
mts; similar, but lower growing, shorter-stemmed. Prostrate
shoots form loose cushions; leaves fleshier, narrower; calyx
more cylindrical.

43

1 *S. dioica*
2 *S. alba*

Fam: CAR.   *Dist:* NW Eur, Br Isles; r in hills of N Scot and Ire.
Hab: c in wds, hbs, on less acid soils. Fl 5–9.

Per, its egg-shaped basal leaves persist through winter; stem hairy, erect, up to 1 m, with pairs of opposite elliptic leaves. In inflorescence stems fork repeatedly with a flower in each fork; upper stem and flower-calyces are glandular-hairy. Flowers have a tubular, ribbed, five-toothed reddish calyx, and five rose-red petals each with a spreading part deeply cleft into two lobes and a stalk; where they join, two small whitish scales. Plants dioecious, males with 10 stamens per flower, females five long styles above an ovary; insect pollination. Ovoid ripe capsule opens by 10 outward-turning teeth at top.

    White Campion, *S. alba*, dioecious, similar, on open banks, ar; not wds; c but rarer to N and W. Flowers white; capsule broader, teeth erect. In both species male calyces 10-veined, female 20-veined.

Fam: CAR. *Dist.* Br Isles and W Eur.
Hab: c in wet mds and wds, fens. Fl 5–7.

This per plant, 30–60 cm tall, has reddish stems, rough above, arising from the creeping rootstock; the stems bear lance-shaped leaves in opposite pairs, stalked below, narrower and stalkless above. Flowers are reminiscent of those of Red Campion, but usually of a brighter rosy red (sometimes white forms occur), with five petals that are each deeply cleft into four narrow segments. As in Red Campion, there are scales where the spreading petal lobes join their narrow stalks. The sepals form a narrow reddish 10-veined calyx-tube, bearing five pointed teeth above. The flowers are bisexual and unscented, with 10 stamens and five styles, and produce neither nectar nor scent. The fruit is a one-celled capsule, opening by five teeth.

COMMON MOUSE-EAR CHICKWEED

Cerastium fontanum

Fam: CAR.   *Dist:* Br Isles and W Eur.
Hab: c in open habs; eg, dunes, ar, downs, wet mds, high mts, hs. Avoids v acid soils. Fl 4–9.

This little plant is readily distinguished from the common ·Chickweed by its hairy stems, and oblong (rather than egg-shaped) leaves. A per (sometimes an) herb, it has a slender creeping rootstock from which arise both creeping flowerless, and erect flowering stems, normally 10–15 cm tall, occasionally more. The whole plant is v hairy; leaves, particularly of the non-flowering shoots, may develop a purplish colour especially in v dry conditions. The repeatedly forked cymose inflorescences bear flowers 8–15 mm across, each with five hairy, ovate, lance-shaped green sepals, with silvery white margins, and five white petals, scarcely longer than the sepals, which are deeply cleft into two lobes. Ten stamens; five styles; the ripe capsule, 9–12 mm long, is curved and cylindrical, opening by 10 teeth to release many tiny brown seeds. The plant has several similar-looking relatives, distinguished by features too complex to consider here.

Fam: CAR.   *Dist:* Br Isles and W Eur.
Hab: very c on cultivated land and wa. Fl 3–12.

This sprawling an plant is one of our commonest weeds. Its diffusely-branched stems bear egg-shaped, pointed leaves in opposite pairs; the upper ones are larger (up to 25 mm long) than the lower ones, and stalkless, while the lower leaves may have long stalks. The leaves are normally hairless except at the base. The repeatedly branched inflorescence is a cyme like that of the Stitchworts, and bears small flowers, about 8 mm across, with hairy ovate green sepals and white, deeply cleft petals normally no longer than the sepals. There are from three to eight stamens and three styles, and the capsule is oblong in shape. Chickweed is not a v pretty plant, but it is a v successful one, that now grows in all temperate regions where European man has taken his farming techniques. It soon disappears, however, where cultivation ceases and coarser per plants can compete with it. If not insect-pollinated, it automatically pollinates itself.

1 *S. holostea*
2 *S. graminea*

Fam: CAR.   *Dist:* c W Eur; Br Isles, not all Scot isles.
Hab: wds, hbs; avoids v acid heathy soils. Fl 4–5.

Delicate per with creeping rootstock from which arise in
spring erect but weak stems that bear stalkless rigid, rough-
edged, lance-shaped leaves in opposite pairs. Star-like white
flowers, up to 25 mm across, are in cymes, which branch
repeatedly in pairs with a flower in each fork. Five narrow
green sepals; five longer petals, deeply cleft halfway into two
lobes; 10 stamens; three styles. Fertilized by small insects,
the ovary swells to a globular green capsule about 6 mm
wide, with many reddish seeds.

Lesser Stitchwort, *S. graminea*, of similar dist, habit and
leaves but softer, more sprawling; usually on lighter, more
acid soils on open gslds or heaths. Flowers about half the size
(up to 12 mm across) of those of Greater Stitchwort; petals
cleft nearly to the base; bracts of the flowers have broad
chaffy margins unlike the wholly green ones of the above
species; leaves have smooth margins. Fl 5–9.

PROCUMBENT PEARLWORT *Sagina procumbens*

1 flower ×2

Fam: CAR.   *Dist:* c in Br Isles and W Eur. Fl 5–10.
Hab: bare pastures, wa, paths, stony lake shores etc.

This little plant is a v low spreading per that tolerates being
trampled on; hence, it tends to be common on paths and
between paving stones. It tends to form mats of rooting
branches only 5–10 cm across, with awl-shaped leaves
joined in pairs at their base. The flowers are minute (2–3 mm
across) and usually have four green hooded sepals, four
stamens and an ovary with four styles. Sometimes (but not
often) four tiny white petals are present. The egg-shaped
capsule is longer than the sepals, which spread in fruit. Like
Shepherd's-purse, it is notably successful under man's
domination of the landscape.

1 shoot-tip ×1

Fam: CHE.   *Dist:* coastal, Br Isles and W Eur.
Hab: salt-marshes, near sea-coasts on tidal estuaries. Fl 9–10.

Glasswort, a strange-looking plant, is an erect an herb with a succulent, pointed stem. It has opposite pairs of similarly succulent branches, which divide again to form a bushy mass. At first green and glossy, it eventually develops a brownish or reddish-purple flush. The individual segments are swollen and convex. Leaves are represented only by small triangular lobes in opposite pairs at upper margins of segments. Flowering is not easy to see. At the apex of the stems small fleshy segments about 1–2 mm across develop in threes; from a pore in the centre of each segment a tiny anther appears. The bifid stigma usually remains hidden inside the pore, but may emerge briefly. The fruits are small nutlets, released when the plant breaks up in winter.

There are several other annual species of Glasswort, difficult to identify, and one per species, Perennial Glasswort, *Arthrocnemum perenne*, with persistent woody stems that form low bushy tussocks up to 1 m across.

Fam: MAL.   *Dist:* c most of W Eur, S Eng; less c to N, and in W Ire.

Hab: c in rds, hbs, wa, dry mds; r in hills. Fl 6–9.

Sparsely-hairy per herb; clusters of spreading or rising stems, up to 80 cm tall; these bear, below, long-stalked, palmate, rounded leaves, and above, more deeply-lobed short-stalked leaves. Flowers, 2·5–4·0 cm across, on short stalks, bright purplish-pink, in clusters in the upper leaf axils. Besides calyx of five triangular green sepals, an epicalyx (extra outer whorl) of three green narrower segments. Petals, notched at tips, have darker purple stripes. The many stamens are joined into a tube below; many styles on a common stalk. The ripe fruit is a whorl of nutlets close-packed round the style.

   Marsh-mallow, *Althaea officinalis*, local in marshes, banks, near sea in E Eng, Ire, W Eur; decreasing. Velvety-leaved, taller, downier; larger pale-rosy pink flowers, no purple veins; epicalyx of eight–nine narrow segments joined below.

Fam: GER.   *Dist:* c in Br Isles, W Eur. Fl 4–9.
Hab: dry banks, dunes, rds, mds; not mts, moors.

An herb with rootstock bearing decumbent or ascending
branches; long soft white hairs on stems and leaves. Basal
leaves on long stalks, kidney-shaped or rounded, irregularly
and bluntly lobed; upper leaves shorter-stalked, more
deeply and sharply lobed. Flowers, 8–12 cm across, are in
loose cymes; five hairy ovate sepals; five bright rosy-purple
petals, notched at the apex. Ten stamens; a stout style
ending in five short purple stigmas. The ripe capsule,
comprising five hairless, wrinkled, one-seeded lobes, opens
by the strip of carpel beak above carrying it upwards by
rolling up to the apex of the style column.

    Small-flowered Crane's-bill, *G. pusillum*, c in similar habs
in Eng and Wales, r in Scot and Ire; smaller, dingy mauve
flowers, 5–8 mm across, with notched petals; downy (not
long-haired) on stems and leaves. Cut-leaved Crane's-bill,
G. dissectum, c, mostly on ar, in Br Isles; more erect; deeply-
cut leaves, hairy stems, spine-tipped sepals, pink petals.

HERB-ROBERT   *Geranium robertianum*

Fam: GER.   *Dist:* Br Isles, W Eur.
Hab: c in wds, hbs, mossy rocks, usually on fairly base-rich soils. Also on stony seashores. Fl 5–9.

This an or bi herb has branched, erect, but straggling, usually red stems, hairy below, shiny above; stems bear, below, attractive bright green palmate leaves, whose lobes are deeply divided pinnately into narrow segments; upper leaves shorter-stalked, with smaller and fewer lobes. The whole plant is rather brittle, with a strong smell which most people would call unpleasant, though to others it is nostalgic of the countryside. Flowers, 10–14 mm across, are in loose cymes, like those of *G. molle*, but have five long-stalked, bright pink wedge-shaped undivided petals, and ovate sharp-pointed erect net-veined, reddish, hairy sepals. Carpels, covered with a network of ridges, have beaks up to 2 cm long.

1 fruits

Fam: GER.   *Dist:* c in all Br Isles; W Eur. Fl 6–9.
Hab: dunes, wa, near sea; o sandy places inland in S.

Low-growing an plant, with basal rosette of hairy, 2–20 cm long, pinnate leaves, with leaflets again much divided. From rosette may spread or ascend hairy stems bearing long-stalked inflorescences of one-nine flowers in terminal umbels. Flowers have five pink, undivided petals, similar to those of Herb-Robert, sometimes with a dark purple spot at the base of the petals. Five pointed green sepals; 10 filaments, of which only five bear anthers on their tips. Five hairy carpels have pink stigmas on top of the stout style column; unripe fruit is stouter and longer than that of Herb-Robert, with a beak up to 40 mm long; when fruit ripens the carpels separate by the style column breaking longitudinally from its axis into five long tail-like strips which remain attached to their one-seeded carpel lobes. The strips bear silky hairs, and as they dry, twist like corkscrews. When they fall, they can screw themselves into loose soil, thus burying the seeds.

Fam: OXA.   *Dist:* more humid parts of Br Isles and W Eur.
Hab: c in dry oak and beech wds; hbs; mts among shady
rocks. Fl 4–5.

A charming and delicate per herb that would be more prized
if rarer. Slender pinkish creeping rhizome bears swollen
scale-like bases, from which arise long-stalked fresh green
trefoil leaves, rather like those of Dutch Clover in size and
form but much more delicate, with three entire drooping
leaflets, bright yellow-green above and purplish below.
Flowers are on 5–10 cm-long, pale yellow-green stalks, with
two tiny bracteoles in the middle. They bear solitary flowers,
10–25 mm across; each has five narrow sepals; five broad
white petals, delicately veined with lilac; 10 stamens; five
styles. Fruit is a hairless five-angled capsule, 3–4 mm long,
which ejects its black seeds forcibly. As in Dog-violet,
inconspicuous flowers, developed in late summer, that do
not open, produce most of the seed.

1 male flower
2 female flower

Fam: AQU. *Dist:* most of Br Isles, especially c in New Forest; r away from coastal NW Eur.
Hab: dry wds, hs; oceanic species.

Usually a shrub, Holly can grow to 20 m tall with a trunk over 1 m in girth. Its thin bark and broad evergreen foliage indicate its lack of adaptation to severe cold. Glossy dark green leaves are spiny on the lower branches, but egg-shaped and untoothed higher up. Holly is dioecious; only female trees produce the scarlet berries. Both male and female trees have white flowers in clusters on older twigs; four petals each, joined below; no separate sepals. Male flowers have four short-stalked stamens; female a single short style. Ripe fruit, technically a drupe rather than a berry, contains three or more stones, each holding one seed. Presumably because, as evergreen, it can photosynthesize in mild winter weather, it can form an understory in beech or oak forests, which let light through after leaf-fall.

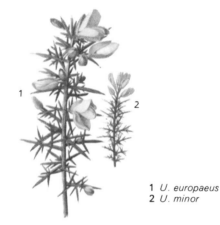

1 *U. europaeus*
2 *U. minor*

Fam: LEG.   *Dist:* Br Isles, except high and in Fens; in W Eur coastal only. Fl all year; peak 4.
Hab: rough gslds, heath; more acid soils.

V spiny evergreen shrub up to 2 m tall. Trifoliate leaves only when young. On mature plants furrowed straight spines formed from short stems, shorter lateral spines from leaf-stalks. Bright yellow coconut-scented flowers, up to 2 cm long; each in axil of a small spine and with ovate bracteoles 3-5 mm long, 2-4 mm wide, on velvety stalks. Calyx of two hairy lobes up to 10 mm long; corolla of five petals, a standard, two wings, two conjoined lower ones forming boat-shaped keel. Stamens joined in a tube. Pod resembles that of Broom, but only 1·5 cm long; pollination, seed dispersal as in Broom.
    Dwarf Gorse, *U. minor*, smaller, on hths in SE Eng and W France. Spines shorter, weaker, smoother; bracteoles 0·5 mm long; darker yellow flowers, fl 8-9. Western Gorse, *U. gallii*, rather larger than *U. minor*, c in W Br Isles; spines stiffer than in Dwarf Gorse, wing petals longer than keel. Fl 8-9.

1 pod

Fam: LEG. *Dist:* Br Isles and W Eur. Fl 5–6.
Hab: open areas on dry, acid, usually sandy soils.

This shrub has long, erect green branches, spineless, hairless
and five-angled, carried in almost parallel fascicles.
Youngest shoots of the current year bear small, long-stalked,
silkily hairy, trifoliate green leaves, lasting one season only;
bright yellow Peaflowers, five-petalled, up to 20 mm long,
borne in pairs or solitary. Ten stamens, joined into a boat-
shaped tube. Calyx small, two-lipped; lower lip three-
toothed, upper two-toothed. A single carpel with a spirally
coiled style within the stamen-tube. Tube itself compressed
within the two keel petals. Large bees break the suture
joining the keel petals and the flower 'explodes' onto the
bee's underside, dusting it with pollen, while the stigma
receives pollen already present on the bee. Fruit is like a
small black hairy-edged Pea-pod, 3–4 cm long, containing
black seeds in a single row. When ripe it bursts into two
valves which coil up suddenly into spirals.

Fam: LEG.   *Dist:* France, Belgium; lowland Br Isles, r in N and W Scot and W Ire. Fl 6–9.
Hab: c on rough gslds, on chalk, limestone, sand (especially fixed dunes).

Low per shrub, with harsh unpleasant smell when handled. Woody rhizomes produce rooting procumbent or ascending stems bearing trifoliate leaves with toothed downy glandular leaflets and leafy basal stipules. Pea-like flowers, 10–15 mm long, in leaf axils in racemes on short stems; pink, darker veined standards and keels, wing petals whitish. Small seed-pod remains enclosed in bell-shaped calyx.

Spiny Restharrow, *O. spinosa*, similar but more erect, with narrower leaflets; stems usually armed with long spines, and with two lines of hairs (not hairy all round as in Common Restharrow which is rarely spiny). Occurs in gslds on heavy clay soils; in the Br Isles almost confined to Eng, where locally c in the S; widespread in similar places in W Eur.

Fam: LEG.   *Dist:* Br Isles except NW and Mid Scot; W Eur.
Hab: dry gslds, rds; not on wet or acid soils, or on mts or moors. Fl 5–8.

Low-growing, spreading or ascending herb, usually an but sometimes a short-lived per. A closely downy plant with trifoliate leaves alternating along stems. Leaves have blunt oval leaflets 5–20 mm long; lance-shaped stipules in pairs where leaf-stalks join stem. Flowers gathered into close globular yellow heads, 5–8 mm across. Individual flowers have Peaflower form characteristic of its family, but are only 2–3 mm long. Fruits are coiled kidney-shaped pods about 2 mm across the coil, with a netted surface; first green, turning black when ripe and not opening.

Hop Trefoil, *Trifolium campestre*, similar but taller; a few hairs, but never closely downy. Pods one-seeded but obovate, straight and brown, enclosed when ripe by the turned-down persistent petals; thus fruiting head resembles a tiny brown hop-head.

1 pod ×1

Fam. LEG.   *Dist:* native probably only SE Eur: natura
lized, f in Br Isles, W Eur; c only in S, mid Eng.
Hab: wa, rds, railways. Fl 7–9.

Upright bi plant, resembling a tall yellow clover with
flowers in long racemes, grows 60–120 cm high; trifoliate
leaves with oblong toothed leaflets and narrow green
stipules. Loose racemes, 4–6 cm long, of tiny (5–6 mm long)
pale yellow Peaflowers, with wings and standard longer than
keel. Oval pods, hairless, bearing transverse ridges; brown
when ripe.

    Tall Melilot, *M. altissima*; of v similar appearance;
probably native on heavy or chalky soils in scrub and wd
borders in S Eng. Most readily distinguished from Ribbed
Melilot by its downy pods, net-marked and black when ripe,
and more pointed: also by its deeper yellow flowers with all
petals of equal length.

1 single flower ×1

Fam: LEG.   *Dist:* Br Isles, W Eur.
Hab: gslds, hbs, rds, both dry and moist. Fl 5–9.

A very c per herb, with hairy, erect stems, up to 60 cm tall, bearing trefoil leaves with toothed elliptic leaflets, dark green, normally with a crescent-shaped pale spot near their base. Stipules up to 10 mm long, triangular, bristle-pointed, with strong brown or purple veins. Flowers in dense globular heads with two leaves just below the top of the peduncle; long narrow corollas, purplish-red in the truly wild form, pink in some cultivated strains grown for hay. Calyx-tube narrowly bell-shaped, ribbed, and with bristle-like teeth shorter than the corolla. Cultivated forms, now often commoner than the native form, also have hollow (not solid) stems and untoothed leaflets.

Fam: LEG.   *Dist:* f in W Eur, S Eng; r northwards to Inverness; in Ire coastal only.
Hab: dry sandy fields, dunes, near sea. Fl 6–9.

Downy erect an Clover, may be 10–30 cm tall. Branching stems bear alternate leaves, each with three narrow leaflets, 10–15 mm long. Stipules at base of each leaf have long bristle-like points. Tiny pinky-white flowers, with v hairy bristle-like calyx teeth, are gathered into cylindrical heads up to 25 mm long on stalks quite as long as the leaves. Pods obovate, only about 1–2 mm long. The dry open places where it grows are good ones to search in June for other, rarer Clovers and other small annual plants that soon disappear in dry summers.

WHITE or DUTCH CLOVER *Trifolium repens*

Fam: LEG.   *Dist:* Br Isles, W Eur. Fl 6–9.
Hab: ab in pastures, rds, on all but v acid soils.

Creeping hairless per herb. Its runners root at the nodes and
bear trifoliate leaves on stalks up to 15 cm long with obovate
leaflets that often have a white inverted V-shaped band near
the base, and pointed green basal stipules. Flowers borne in
globular heads on peduncles 5–10 cm long; narrow corollas,
white, sometimes pink-tinged. Each flower has a pedicel 2–
4 mm long. Calyx-tube is bell-shaped with narrow long
teeth, and is white with green veins. In fruit corollas fold
over the pods, which are 4–5 mm long and contain several
seeds. This plant is one of the most important fodder plants
and is frequently sown in ley pastures mixed with such
grasses as Rye Grass (*Lolium perenne* or *L. multiflorum*).

1 flower ×1

Fam: LEG. *Dist:* c in Br Isles, W Eur. Fl 5–9.
Hab: calcareous gslds, fixed dunes, rocks near sea.

Attractive Peaflowered downy per up to 60 cm tall (but usually much less and often prostrate on ground); silky pinnate leaves with few pairs of leaflets. In lower leaves the terminal leaflet is elliptic and much larger than others; in the upper, all leaflets equal-sized and narrow. Stalks of upper leaves v short; stipules like the leaflets but smaller. Flower-heads are in pairs at the top of the stems, with leaflets arising below them. Each flower has a membranous calyx, tubular and densely white-woolly. Corolla normally yellow, protrudes a few mm from the calyx-tube; in some coastal sites, flowers may be white, pink, cream, purple or crimson; a particularly beautiful display of colour forms may be seen near Kynance Cove in S Cornwall. In fruit, the globular netted one-seeded pods remain enclosed within the inflated, now straw-coloured calyx.

COMMON BIRD'S-FOOT-TREFOIL

Lotus corniculatus

Fam: LEG.   *Dist:* c in Br Isles, W Eur.
Hab: downlands, old pastures. Fl 5–9.

This bright yellow-flowered little Trefoil has a woody per
rootstock, producing several trailing branched stems. These
bear normally hairless leaves with three egg-shaped pointed
leaflets at the tip of the stalk, and a similar pair just above
where it joins the stem. The stipules are minute and brown.
The flowers, about 15 mm long, are borne in heads, and are
spread out in a semicircle on the tips of 8 cm-long peduncles
set in leaf axils. Buds are deep red, flattened, vaguely
resembling rashers of bacon. As they are mixed with the egg-
yolk-coloured open flowers, the plant is sometimes called
Bacon-and-Eggs. The pods, of which three or four usually
develop on each stalk, are 2–3 cm long, and spread out at
right angles to the common stalk or peduncle like the toes of
a bird's foot. The tiny green calyx has five acute teeth; and
there are several seeds in each pod.

HORSESHOE VETCH   *Hippocrepis comosa*

1 pods ×0·5

Fam: LEG.   *Dist:* locally c in Eng S of Kendal; r in Wales.
C in France, S Belgium, S Germany.
Hab: old gslds, rocks, on chalk and limestone. Fl 5–7

A low-growing, per herb with woody rootstock bearing
many branching stems, procumbent or rising to about 15 cm
high. Pinnately compound leaves, normally bearing four or
five pairs of narrowly-oblong blunt hairless leaflets and a
similar terminal leaflet. No tendrils; narrow pointed stipules
at base of each leaf. Flowers bright yellow, five–eight
together, in whorls on ends of 6–10 cm stalks or peduncles.
Flowers Pea-like, resembling those of Bird's-foot-trefoil, but
narrower, clearer yellow, about 10 mm long. Sinuous pods,
about 30 mm long, break into horseshoe-shaped segments
when ripe, giving plant its name. With Horseshoe Vetch
there may also occur interesting chalk plants, such as some of
the Orchids.

Fam: LEG.   *Dist:* Br Isles, NW Eur.
Hab: c in hs, wd borders, drier fens. Fl 6–8.

Climbing per Vetch, with creeping rhizomes that produce
scrambling stems which may climb to a height of 2 m or
more up other vegetation by means of their leaf tendrils.
Each leaf is 10–25 mm long, pinnate, with up to about 12
pairs of leaflets which are narrow and downy, on the
underside especially; and have narrow basal stipules. At the
apex of each leaf there is a tendril which bears one or two side
branches. The racemes of flowers are pinkish-purple in bud,
but bright blue-purple when open, and 10–12 mm long. The
pods, like tiny Peas 10–20 mm long, are hairless and have up
to six seeds in each.

Fam: LEG.   *Dist:* c in Br Isles, NW Eur. Fl 5–8.
Hab: wds, hbs; in open places more in W and N.

A nearly hairless per, it may climb to a height of 1 m, but
frequently trails over the ground or low vegetation. Leaves
have six–nine pairs of oval leaflets, usually rather blunt and
much broader than those of Tufted Vetch (but the stipules
are half arrow-shaped in both); branched tendrils on leaf-
tips. The flowers are pale rosy-purple, not bluish; and are
wider and longer (up to 15 mm) than in Tufted Vetch, and
occur in much shorter racemes with short peduncles. The
ripe pods are up to 25 mm long and are beaked and black
when ripe.

COMMON VETCH   *Vicia sativa*

1 pod ×0·5

Fam: LEG.   *Dist:* Br Isles except NW Scot; W Eur.
Hab: c in hs, scrub, old gslds. Fl 5–9.

This occurs in two forms: one native with narrow linear
leaflets, often known as *V. angustifolia*, and one with oblong
blunt leaflets, of cultivated origin but commonly naturalized
(*V. sativa* proper). A hairy tufted sprawling or climbing an
herb, its stems bear pinnate leaves with three–eight pairs of
leaflets; at the tip of each a tendril, perhaps branched, which
twines around other plants. Peaflowers, 15–20 mm long, are
singly or in pairs in the upper leaves' axils; pale purple in *V.
sativa*, but often deep purple and smaller in the native form.
The five calyx-teeth are as long as the calyx-tube. As in all
Leguminosae, each flower has five petals; a standard at the
back, two narrower wings at each side, and two partly joined
by their lower edges below and in front that form the boat-
shaped keel. The 10 stamens are partially joined into a tube
round the single carpel. Pods are 25–70 mm long, like small
Peapods, usually downy, and turn brown or black when
ripe.

70

Fam: LEG.   *Dist:* Br Isles and W Eur.
Hab: c in hs, mds, scrub and wd borders. Fl 5–8.

This climbing Peaflower is a per, with scrambling, some-times finely downy stems and leaves. The angled weak stem, up to 120 cm tall, but usually much less, bears leaves which have only two 1–3 cm-long, rigid lance-shaped leaflets with strong parallel veins running lengthwise, and usually a branched terminal tendril. The two stipules at the base of the leaf are arrow-shaped and broader than the leaflets. The flowers are borne in long-stalked racemes of five–twelve flowers together. The Pea-like pods are up to 35 mm long and have up to 10 seeds in each.

   Several other species of *Lathyrus* occur wild; the Narrow-leaved Everlasting-pea, *L. sylvestris*, is a much larger plant with rose-pink yellow-suffused flowers and narrow leaflets up to 15 cm long, that scrambles over hds and in open wds locally in GB (not in Ire) N to Angus.

Fam: ROS.   *Dist:* Br Isles and W Eur. Fl late 6–9.
Hab: ab in fens, marshy mds, wet wds, riversides, wet rock ledges in mt areas; not in v acid bogs.

This per herb has stems up to 120 cm tall, erect, often reddish-tinged. Dark green leaves, pinnate, with deeply-toothed ovate leaflets, pairs of larger ones (up to 8 cm long) alternating up the leaf-stalk with pairs of tiny ones (1–4 mm long). Terminal leaflet usually three-lobed. Round leafy-toothed stipules at base of each leaf. Leaflets, normally white-woolly below, may be green and hairless. Tiny cream-coloured flowers, 4–6 mm across, gathered in large numbers in round-topped dense corymbs of irregular form at the stem apices; sweetly-scented, but produce no nectar. Each flower has a four- or five-lobed calyx, and a corolla of five or six petals with long stalks. The many stamens protrude and surround the six–ten green carpels which twist together spirally, forming one-seeded achenes when ripe.

BLACKBERRY or BRAMBLE   *Rubus fruticosus*

Fam: ROS.   *Dist:* Br Isles except high mts; W Eur.
Hab: ab in wds, hs, hths, scrublands. Fl 6–9.

The per rootstock produces stout, usually arching stems
which may climb over other shrubs or bend down to earth
and root there, forming new plants. Stems are variously
armed with prickles, hooked spines and hairs, which may be
gland-tipped. The species is extremely variable, in reality
consisting of many sub-species (nearly 400 in the Br Isles
alone) distinguished by the different types of stem armament
and hairs, leaf shape, flower colour, fruit form, colour and
flavour, etc. Leaves are compound, with usually three–five
oval or oblong leaflets arranged palmately; prickles and
hairs are found in varying degrees on the leaflets and their
stalks. Flowers either white or pink, in loose panicles on the
ends of branches from the last year's stems. Calyx forms a
five-lobed cup; five separate, often crinkly, petals; many
stamens. Numerous carpels, grouped on a conical receptacle; each contains two ovules, only one of which forms
a seed. Fruits, black or reddish, are aggregations of little
fleshy drupes cohered together on receptacle.

Fam: ROS.   *Dist:* W Eur; Br Isles, except NW Scot and the outer islands. Fl 2–5.
Hab: hbs, open wds, dry scrubby gslds.

This little plant is very reminiscent of the Wild Strawberry. Its per tufted rootstock produces only short stolons (not long runners as in Strawberries); trifoliate long-stalked leaves like those of Wild Strawberry in general form, but silky and dull bluish-green (not glossy green) and broadly obovate, with their terminal tooth shorter than those on either side of it (in Wild Strawberry the leaflets are more pointed, with the terminal tooth the longest). The few-flowered panicles bear small white flowers; notched, widely separated petals, scarcely longer than the sepals. An epicalyx is present, as in the Strawberry. Many stamens and carpels; the receptacle carrying these does not swell up in fruit to become red and juicy, but remains dry and hard.

Fam: ROS.   *Dist:* c throughout Br Isles and W Eur.
Hab: damp rds, damp mds, moist sandy hollows in dunes.
Fl 6–8.

This widespread plant may be easily recognized by the silky
hairs especially on the undersides of the leaves, which give
the foliage a silvery white appearance. Its creeping runners
produce pinnate leaves, 5–10 cm long, which bear deeply
toothed leaflets. Between the larger leaflets there are tiny
ones, an arrangement also found in Meadowsweet. Flowers
are large for the plant, 1·5–2 cm across, with five golden
yellow petals, five green sepals, and five bracteoles outside
the sepals, forming what is called an epicalyx. (This, present
here as in all the species of *Potentilla*, helps in distinguishing
the yellow-flowered *Potentillae* from the Buttercups, which
are without it). Numerous stamens and carpels.

Fam: ROS.   *Dist:* Br Isles and W Eur.
Hab: c on hths, acid gslds at all altitudes. Not on chalk or limestone except where there are deposits of superficial non-calcareous soil. Fl 6–9.

Tormentil is another small herb of the Rose family with yellow flowers superficially resembling those of Buttercups. Its stems are tufted and branched, either erect (to 10 cm tall) or trailing shortly over Heather and grasses; it lacks the long stolons of Creeping Cinquefoil. Leaves, 2–3 cm across, shiny green and almost hairless, are digitate (five-fingered) as in Creeping Cinquefoil, but, apart from the basal leaves, are sessile (without stalks) and each one bears a pair of stipules like two smaller leaflets at the base. Flowers, in the axils of the leaves, are on stalks 2–4 cm long and are smaller than those of Creeping Cinquefoil (1–1·5 cm across); they have normally only four petals and four sepals, not five of each.

CREEPING CINQUEFOIL   *Potentilla reptans*

Fam: ROS.   *Dist:* lowlands of Br Isles and W Eur
Hab: c on rds, wa. Fl 6–9.

From the woody rootstock of this low-growing plant extend
creeping stems, often 50–100 cm long, which root at intervals. From these arise leaves on stalks 3–8 cm long with
five oval to elliptical leaflets arranged like spreading fingers
(digitate). These leaflets are toothed, broadest above the
middle, and sparingly hairy. The flowers are about 2·0–
2·5 cm across, bright yellow, and borne singly on stalks up to
8 cm-long in the leaf axils. There are five yellow petals, five
shorter green sepals which alternate with the petals, and an
epicalyx (see Silverweed). Stamens and carpels are numerous in the centre of the flower.

Fam: ROS.   *Dist:* Br Isles and W Eur.
Hab: c on hbs, scrub, open wds, on all except strongly acid or waterlogged soils. Fl 5–7.

The Wild Strawberry v much resembles a miniature garden Strawberry. The woody rootstock is per and from this arise both flowering shoots and long runners. The basal leaves of the flowering shoots have hairy stalks 3–5 cm long, each bearing three oval leaflets which are hairy but of a rather shining bright green, unlike the dull grey-green leaves of Barren Strawberry. These leaflets have strong side veins, and they are broadest above the middle, with sharp teeth, and (again unlike Barren Strawberry) the terminal tooth is longer than those next to it on each side. The reddish-coloured runners root at intervals, forming new plants with tufts of leaves. The flowers are borne in a loose inflorescence about 5–10 cm tall, and are white and 1·5–2 cm across, with five broad blunt petals, five narrow green sepals and a five-lobed epicalyx. There are numerous stamens and carpels. In fruit the receptacle swells to form the familiar red strawberry which is up to 2 cm long, with the tiny achenes dotted over its surface.

1 *G. urbanum*
2 *G. rivale*

Fam: ROS.   *Dist:* Br Isles and W Eur. Fl 5–8.
Hab: c in less acid wds and hbs; moist rich soils.

Per herb; stems up to 60 cm tall. Root-leaves have rounded, coarse-toothed terminal leaflet, 5 cm wide; two–three pairs lateral leaflets, 5 10 mm long. Stem-leaves have three equal, simple leaflets. Stipules large, leafy, toothed. Flowers few, erect, long-stalked in open cymes; five spreading yellow petals; five green sepals; five-lobed epicalyx. Many stamens, and hairy carpels with long, double-bent styles breaking at bend when ripe to form hook by which achenes attach to animals for dispersal.

  Water Avens, *G. rivale*, similar, in moister hab, c in N Br Isles, local in S; f W Eur. Terminal leaflets of root-leaves, up to 10 cm wide, less deeply-toothed; drooping flowers with erect, stalked, orange-pink petals; purplish calyces. Hybridize together.

1 fruit ×1

Fam: ROS.   *Dist:* c in W Eur, Br Isles, but rarer in N Scot.
Fl 6–9.
Hab: rds, hbs, scrubby gslds, especially on chalk.

An upright, hairy, per herb, 30–60 cm tall, with branched
stems, and pinnate leaves up to 15 cm long below, shorter
above. As in many Rosaceae, there are pairs of tiny rounded
leaflets between the larger pairs of lance-shaped toothed
ones, and the pairs of stipules at the leaf bases resemble
leaflets. Flowers in long terminal spiked racemes. Each
flower has five yellow petals 3–4 mm long, five green sepals,
10–20 stamens and two carpels, each with a terminal style.
Each flower has a top-shaped receptacle in whose hollowed-
out interior the carpels sit. Receptacle is grooved externally,
and covered with hooked spines. It enlarges and hardens to
form a bur-like fruit, which is dispersed by catching its now
woody spines on fur, feathers, clothes, etc.

LADY'S-MANTLE *Alchemilla vulgaris*

1 single flower ×1

Fam: ROS. *Dist:* c in Denmark and north of GB, r in the south of GB and of W Eur. Fl 5–9.
Hab: mds, wds, limestone or other basic rocks.

This attractive plant is a per with a stout rootstock bearing tufts of erect or trailing leafy stems. Long-stalked root-leaves are of rounded palmate form with from five to eleven lobes, toothed, green on both sides, and with strong veins. They may be v hairy or almost hairless, but always have hairs on the tips of the teeth. Stem-leaves similar, but smaller and shorter-stalked. Inflorescence, up to 30 cm tall, is an irregularly-branched cyme bearing clusters of small green flowers which have no petals but four tiny sepals up to 2 mm long and an epicalyx of four lobes. Four stamens and one carpel in each flower. Nowadays the Lady's-mantle is divided into about 10 species, differing in the shapes and hairiness of the leaves and their habit, but these distinctions are too complex for discussion here.

Fam: ROS.   *Dist:* c in Eng, Wales, S Ire, W Eur; r in Scot.
Hab: chalky gslds. Fl 5–8.

A per herb with a basal rosette of pinnate leaves up to 8 cm
long; the erect branched stem, usually 15–30 cm tall, bears
similar but smaller alternately-arranged leaves. Leaflets are
shortly oval or round, short-stalked, deeply toothed, and in
opposite pairs on the leaf-stalks; also a terminal leaflet.
Slender stems are terminated by globular heads of tiny
flowers, 7–12 mm across. In each head lowest flowers are
male, with many long stamens; middle ones have both
stamens and carpels; uppermost each have two purple,
brush-like styles. No petals, but all flowers have a four-lobed
green calyx. Pollination is by wind; self-pollination is
unlikely because male and female flowers on an individual
plant mature at different times. The leaves are edible and
have a pleasant sharp taste, rather like cucumber.

DOG ROSE   *Rosa canina*

Fam: ROS.   *Dist:* S of Br Isles, and France.
Hab: lis, scrub, wds. Fl 6–8.

Dog Rose is a shrub with strong, arching stems with curved
spines, up to 3 m tall. Leaves bear several pairs of opposite,
normally simply-toothed leaflets, and a larger terminal
leaflet. All are pointed, and may be hairless or downy below.
Flowers, borne a few together in loose panicles, are sweet-
scented, up to 5 cm across, each with five notched petals,
normally pink but sometimes white. Five narrow green
sepals, which tend to have pinnately arranged side-lobes.
Numerous stamens; many hairy styles, each attached to a
separate little achene within the cup-like receptacle, protrude from it. When the fruit or 'hip' develops, the
receptacle becomes red and fleshy.

  The Field Rose, *R. arvensis*, with its white flowers and
weakly prickly trailing stems, is c in S Eng on heavy soils.
Other species, with often darker pink flowers, and more
gland-covered leaves may be found further N.

OPPOSITE-LEAVED GOLDEN-SAXIFRAGE

Chrysosplenium oppositifolium

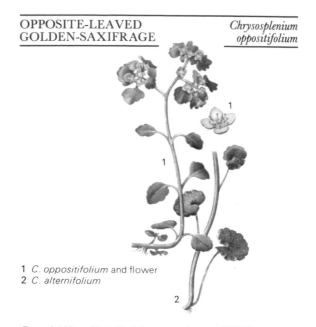

1 *C. oppositifolium* and flower
2 *C. alternifolium*

Fam: SAX.   *Dist:* Br Isles, coastal areas NW Eur.
Hab: c in springy wds; mls; by streams. Fl 4–5.

Small per herb with conspicuous (except 6–8) mats of green foliage; creeping, rooting, brittle stems bear many pairs opposite rounded leaves, stalked, wedge-shaped below, with bristles. Stems erect, 5–15 cm tall, carry repeatedly forked umbel-like cymes of tiny golden flowers surrounded by large greenish-yellow bracts. Nectar present; yellow usually four-toothed calyx; no petals; eight tiny stamens; two conjoined carpels.

Alternate-leaved G-s, *C. alternifolium*, mostly in E and central GB; c in W Eur away from coast; not Ire, W Eng, or Scot. Taller; no creeping leafy stems but leafless stolons. Basal leaves long-stalked, kidney-shaped, 1–2·5 cm across; stem leaves solitary not opposite. Flowers similar; golden sheen on bracts.

Fam: DRO.   *Dist:* Br Isles and W Eur.
Hab: only on wet peat or *Sphagnum* bogs. Fl 6–7.

Small per herb with rosette of spreading basal leaves, 2–5 cm long with their stalks. Each has an almost circular green blade up to 1 cm across, covered and fringed with stalked red glands. From centre of rosette arise a few slender stems, 10–15 cm tall; these branch above to bear two rows of tiny white flowers, about 5 mm across; five or six rounded petals; several stamens. Flowers open in turn for a few hours on sunny mornings only. Tiny capsules, each producing many seeds. Sundew traps insects as on fly-paper by the sticky secretion of the gland-tipped red leaf-hairs. The outer longer hairs slowly enclose the trapped insect, and then the protein in it is dissolved and absorbed into the plant, perhaps mainly to supplement its nitrogen supply. There are two other, rarer, species.

PURPLE-LOOSESTRIFE   *Lythrum salicaria*

Fam: LYT.   *Dist:* W Eur, Ire, south of GB; r in N Scot.
Fl 6–9.
Hab: c in swamps, marshes, fens, river banks.

Its creeping rootstocks produce erect, angled stems, 60–
120 cm tall, bearing opposite or three-whorled sessile,
usually downy, lanceolate untoothed leaves, 4–7 cm long
with clasping bases. Stems, simple or branched, terminate
in spike-like inflorescences up to 30 cm long; many purple
flowers in whorls in axils of leafy bracts. Flowers, up to
20 mm across, have four to (usually) six oblong petals: calyx
a 12-toothed pubescent ribbed tube; 12 stamens; a two-
celled ovary (enclosed in but free from the calyx) develops
into an ovoid capsule. Species is trimorphic, having three
sorts of flower, borne each on different plants; some have
short styles, long stamens; some medium styles, short and
long stamens; some long styles, short and medium stamens.
The size of the pollen grains also differs in the three types.

ROSEBAY WILLOWHERB *Epilobium angustifolium*

Fam: ONA.   *Dist:* W Eur, c south of GB, much of Scot; o in Ire. Fl 7–9.
Hab: wa, open or felled wds, rocky places, railways.

Its per creeping rootstocks bear erect leafy stems, 30–120 cm tall, almost glabrous, and bearing lance-shaped spirally-arranged leaves, 5–15 cm long, on short stalks shaped rather like those of some Willows. Flowers, 2–3 cm across, in dense racemes. Each flower has four rose-purple petals, of which two broader ones are above and two narrower spread horizontally (not in the form of an equal-armed cross). Four narrow purple sepals; eight stamens; four stigmas on a long style. The inferior ovary develops after fertilization into a purple four-angled downy capsule, 2·5–8 cm long, which eventually splits to release numerous seeds, each with a white parachute-plume of hairs for wind dispersal. No stigma spreads until the pollen of its own flower has been shed, thus avoiding self-pollination.

1 flower ×1

Fam: ONA.   *Dist:* c Br Isles and W Eur. Fl 6–8.
Hab: c in wds on base-rich soils; wa; shady gardens.

The stems of this per herb rise from creeping rootstocks, by which the plant increases vegetatively. Stems are rounded and bear pairs of opposite, long-stalked, oval leaves which are often slightly heart-shaped, faintly toothed, and usually 4–6 cm long. Usually the stems and leaves are slightly downy. Flowers are borne in long racemes, with usually some side racemes in the axils of the upper leaves as well as a terminal one. Two pink-white petals, 2–4 mm long, notched to at least half-way; two green sepals; two stamens; a two-celled ovary, which is inferior to the sepals and petals. The ripe fruit is egg-shaped, about 3 mm across, and contains two cells, each with a single seed. It is covered with hooked white bristles which adhere to animal fur or human clothing and so become dispersed.

Fam: LOR.   *Dist:* f in S and W Eng; r in Wales; absent in Scot and Ire. Westerly in W Eur.
Hab: parasitic on various trees, especially Apple, Hawthorn, Lime, Poplar. Fl 2–4.

Evergreen shrub, familiar as a decoration at Christmas time. Its seeds germinate in the crevices of the bark of trees, normally after passing through the gut of a berry-eating bird; suckers are produced which penetrate the wood, absorbing nutriment from the host tree. It is not, however, a total parasite, as its green leaves can manufacture organic food by photosynthesis. Its branches have a smooth yellow bark, and are repeatedly forked. The oblong, leathery leaves with parallel veins occur in pairs or threes at the tips of the shoots. The tiny flowers are of separate sexes, and usually on separate plants; they occur in small clusters in the forks of the branches. The male flowers have a whorl of four tiny petals and four short stamens; the female a single stigma on a one-celled ovary which develops below the four-lobed calyx and corolla. The fruit, which takes more than a year to develop, consists of a waxy white berry containing a single seed.

1 flowering stem
2 creeping stem
3 fruits

Fam: ARA.   *Dist:* c in Br Isles and W Eur. Fl 9–11.
Hab: climber on trees, rocks, walls; may carpet ground in v
shady wds; absent only on v acid, dry or wet soils.

Climbing shrub, with stems which may reach 25 cm across
and considerable age; they attach themselves to a support
not by twining or tendrils, but by numerous small sucker-
like roots, which are, however, not parasitic. Evergreen
leaves on creeping or lower climbing stems, palmately three-
to five-lobed, with triangular untoothed lobes, and usually
pale veins on a glossy dark green background. Leaves of the
higher, flowering branches are undivided and oval or
elliptic. Creeping stems never flower; flowers, only produced in good light at top of the ascended tree or wall, are in
umbels; five small sepals; five yellow-green triangular petals
3–4 mm long; five short stamens; a single style with a five-
celled inferior ovary. Black globular berries, 6–8 mm across.
Main pollinators are wasps and flies.

1 three fruits

Fam: UMB.   *Dist:* Br Isles and W Eur; also f in mts of tropical Africa and Asia.

Hab: c in woods, especially Beech on chalk; also Oak on base-rich loams and clays. Fl 5–8.

Attractive per herb, has hairless root-leaves, rather like those of Ivy but more deeply three- to five-lobed, sharply toothed, and 2–6 cm across, often obvious on the bare floors of beechwoods in winter. In spring the rootstock produces smooth stems 20–60 cm tall, which bear shorter-stalked, more divided leaves and loose umbels formed of clusters of light few-flowered partial umbels on long stalks, which arise from a whorl of narrow, toothed bracts. Individual flowers are 1–2 mm across, pink or white; the outer ones in each partial umbel have only stamens, while the inner are hermaphrodite. The fruits consist of two rounded carpels covered with hooked spines, and are dispersed by animals to which they adhere. All Umbellifers have the same basic flower structure.

1 *E. maritimum*
2 *E. campestre*

Fam: UMB.   *Dist:* sandy coasts of Br Isles; W Eur seaboard
Portugal to Norway; Baltic shores. Fl 7–9.
Hab: sandy, sometimes shingly beaches, dunes.

A hairless branched per herb, 30–60 cm tall, with v deep
tap-roots, also creeping rhizomes. Intensely glaucous bright
blue-grey leaves, thick-edged with spinous teeth. Root-
leaves long-stalked, almost circular; stem-leaves stalkless,
palmate. Simple umbellate flower-heads, oval, 2·5–4 cm
long, contain close-packed flowers of glorious electric blue.
Five petals, five purplish-pink stamens, two carpels forming
inferior ovary. Each head surrounded by whorl of wedge-
shaped shiny bracts; spines among flowers; hooked spines on
fruits. At first sight looks like Thistle, but flower structure is
that of Umbellifers.

   Field Eryngo, *E. campestre*, very c on rds, dry banks in
France, Low Countries; very r S Eng; slenderer, more
branched; leaves longer, pinnate, grey-green; narrower
heads of mauve-white flowers.

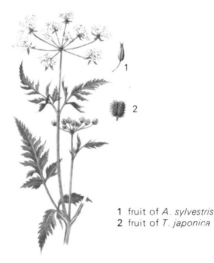

1 fruit of *A. sylvestris*
2 fruit of *T. japonica*

Fam: UMB. *Dist:* lowland Br Isles and W Eur. *Hab:* ab on rds, hbs. Fl 5–6.

Upright bi herb; has hollow furrowed stem, downy below, hairless above, up to 100 cm tall. Leaves lacy, up to 30 cm long, two–three times pinnate, with deeply-cut leaflets. Stem bears several compound umbels of white flowers, sometimes pink-tinged. Base of compound umbel bractless; several bracteoles below flower-heads in the small simple umbel on its branches form green spreading or turned down ruff of narrow segments. Five petals, white with turned-in point; no sepals; five stamens; two styles. Fruits smooth, ovoid, shortly-beaked.

Rough Chervil, *Chaerophyllum temulentum*, c in similar habs; fl 6–7. Solid, purple-spotted stems; dull grey-green, hairy leaves; fruits smooth, narrower below. Upright Hedge-parsley, *Torilis japonica*, c on rds; fl 7–8; smaller umbels; hooked spines on oval fruits.

GOUTWEED or GROUND-ELDER

Aegopodium podagraria

1 stem section

Fam: UMB.   *Dist:* c W Eur; Br Isles (probably as an introduction) except parts of NW Scot.
Hab: gardens, wa; o in woods. Fl 5–7.

Though quite a pretty plant in flower, Goutweed, so-named because of its former medicinal use in treating the complaint, is one of the most pernicious weeds of gardens. A stout upright hairless per herb, up to 1 m tall, with numerous far-creeping fleshy underground rhizomes, it is almost ineradicable when once established; fragments of rhizome always escape removal and form new plants. Leaves light green, triangular, normally twice pinnate, up to 20 cm long, with egg-shaped, pointed, toothed leaflets. Umbels 2–6 cm across and compound, normally without bracts or bracteoles. Flowers white, five-petalled with no calyx; five stamens; two styles and an ovary below the whorl of petals.

HEMLOCK WATER-DROPWORT

Oenanthe crocata

1 flower ×1

Fam: UMB. *Dist:* W and S of GB; Ire; in France S of Somme valley; r or absent in E of GB and N Eur.
Hab: ab in ditches, marshy wds, swamps, especially on clay; avoids chalky and acid soils. Fl 6–7.

Hemlock Water-dropwort is one of the most poisonous of our plants. It is sometimes eaten in mistake for celery, because the leaves are rather similar, with occasionally fatal consequences. It is a tall stout per herb, 50–150 cm tall, with spindle-shaped root-tubers which are the most poisonous part, although they apparently taste sweet. Stems are hollow, ridged and hairless, and bear leaves of triangular outline up to 40 cm long, that are several times pinnately divided with wedge-shaped, coarsely-toothed leaflets. The leaf-stalks sheath the stem. The compound umbels are 5–10 cm across, on the ends of the branches, and have up to 40 primary rays. Many narrow bracts and bracteoles in the umbels. Flowers are white, five-petalled, about 2 mm across.

1 flower ×1
2 fruit ×1
3 stem section
4 leaf-stalk section

Fam: UMB.   *Dist:* Br Isles and W Eur. Fl 7–9.
Hab: marshes, ditches, riversides; wet non-acid wds.

Per herb up to 2 m tall; stout hairless hollow stems, usually purple-tinged. Triangular basal leaves up to 60 cm long, two or three times pinnate with oval leaflets 2–8 cm long. Their stalks, channelled above, expand into inflated sheaths where they join stem. Stem-leaves are similar, smaller up the stem, less divided. Umbels compound, up to 15 cm across; many downy rays bearing simple umbels. Flowers white to pink; five nearly equal petals with turned-in tips; no calyx; five stamens; two carpels below flower. Fruit is two compressed oval carpels, each edged with vertical winged ridges and three dorsal ridges. Its stems and those of Garden Angelica, *A. archangelica*, can be candied to make a sweetmeat.

1 flower ×1

Fam: UMB.   *Dist:* much of W Eur; c in S Eng; r in Wales; if found in Scot or Ire is an escape.
Hab: rds, grassy scrubland, wa; especially on chalk and limestone. Fl 6–8.

Wild Parsnip is a per herb with a strong tap-root. The cultivated Parsnip has been derived from it by selective breeding to make the root much more fleshy. Its erect downy stems are branched, 40–150 cm tall, and hollow with angled furrows along them. Leaves rough and simply pinnate, with egg-shaped but lobed and toothed segments. If handled in bright sunshine ultra-violet light makes the skin sensitive to the plant, and large blisters may develop. Flowers, yellow, with five petals, are in umbels, which are again divided into smaller umbels. The main umbels are 4–10 cm across. Individual flowers only about 1·5 mm across; no calyx. The two-celled fruits are 5–8 mm long, egg-shaped and flattened, and there are five stamens.

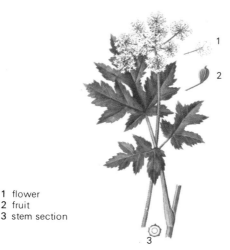

1 flower
2 fruit
3 stem section

Fam: UMB.   *Dist:* Br Isles and W Eur. Fl 6–9.
Hab: ab on rds, wa, hbs, open wds on less acid soil; mt ledges on basic soils. Avoids high moors.

A tall coarse per herb up to 2 m high, with stout, grooved, roughly hairy hollow stem. The rough leaves are simply pinnate but the leaflets are deeply lobed and toothed around edges. Basal leaves may be up to 1 m long. All leaves have broad expanded clasping bases. The stem branches to bear several large compound umbels of white flowers. Umbels, up to 15 cm across, have up to about 20 stout rays. Each ray bears a secondary umbel of white or pinkish flowers; it has narrow bracteoles below. Outer flowers of the main head are larger, with v unequal petals, creating a fringe of longer petals all round the main umbel. Five deeply notched petals to each flower. The two-carpelled ovary develops into an egg-shaped, flattened but bi-convex fruit. The two carpels separate, but each remains suspended by a fibre from the tip of the style.

WILD CARROT   *Daucus carota*

1 fruit ×0·5

Fam: UMB.   *Dist.* lowlands of W Eur and Br Isles; r in N Scot. Fl 6–9
Hab: c in fields, downs, rds, especially on chalk or near sea; r on uplands, moors, mts.

The ancestor of our cultivated carrots, it is an upright roughly hairy bi herb, usually 30–100 cm tall; low-growing more spreading forms f on coasts. Solid ridged stem, branched; bears leaves that are three times pinnate with narrow toothed segments. Flat or rounded compound umbels of white flowers, in fruit become hollow and concave. Each compound umbel has at its base conspicuous pinnately-divided bracts with narrow segments. Smaller, narrower bracteoles below the simple umbels. Individual florets have notched petals with turned-in points; petals of outer flowers of each umbel are usually larger on their outsides. Central flower of compound umbel usually dark red or purple, unique in Umbellifers. Fruits oval, about 3–4 mm long; two carpels, each bearing seven vertical ridges, four armed with long hooked spines that catch on animals for dispersal.

1 *B. cretica* ssp *dioica*
2 *T. communis*

Fam: CUC.   *Dist:* SW Eur, Eng S of Yorks; r Wales.
Hab: hs, scrub, on calcareous or sandy soil. Fl 5–9.

Climbing per herb; from large tuberous rootstock arise
trailing bristly stems bearing palmately lobed, stalked leaves
and (from bases of leaf-stalks) spirally-coiled simple tendrils.
Flowers in axillary clusters. Dioecious; males produce
three–eight greenish stalked flowers, each 12–18 mm across;
five narrow sepals; five net-veined hairy petals; two pairs
short fused stamens, one free stamen. Female flowers slightly
smaller, stalkless, with three bifid stigmas; ovaries develop
below calyx into red berries.

Black Bryony, *Tamus communis*, unrelated climbing herb of
similar dist. A monocotyledon of the Yam family, Dioscorea-
ceae, has per tuberous rootstock; glossy heart-shaped leaves;
six-petalled greenish bell-shaped flowers; dioecious, with six
stamens in male flower, three stigmas in female. Red berries.

1 male plant with
  catkins
2 female flower

Fam: EUP.   *Dist:* W Eur; GB except NW Scot, Scottish
Isles, Isle of Man; r in Ire, probably introduced.
Hab: wds, on base-rich or calcareous soil; rocks and mt
ledges. Fl 2–4.

A per herb, with far-creeping rhizomes that produce massed
stands of erect downy shoots 15–40 cm tall. Stems, unbranched, bear, in opposite pairs, elliptic or lance-shaped
downy leaves, short-stalked, and toothed along their edges.
Plants are dioecious. Males bear long catkin-like spikes of
tiny flowers in the leaf-axils; each flower has three green
sepals, 2 mm long, and eight–fifteen stamens. Females
(which often have wider leaves) bear one–three flowers on
long stalks in the upper leaf-axils; three sepals; ovary ripens
to a hairy two-celled fruit about 6–8 mm wide.

   Annual Mercury, *M. annua*, is c in SE Eng and in France
on wa and ar; more r to N and W; a similar looking but
hairless annual branched plant with unstalked female
flowers and bristly fruits.

1 flower cluster ×1

Fam: EUP.   *Dist:* S Eng; Wales, S of Denbigh; SW Eur.
Hab: broad-leaved wds, except on v acid soil. Fl 3–6.

In winter, low shrub; stout reddish, tufted, 20–30 cm stems;
terminal rosettes of blunt lanceolate downy leaves. In spring
stems bear branched inflorescences, 40–80 cm tall, of compound umbels of tiny green flowers. Whorl of oval bracts
below main umbel; rounded, paired yellowish-green bracts
below each flower cluster. Each ultimate cluster comprises
one tiny three-styled female flower with a globular three-
celled ovary; one-stamened male flowers around it. Tiny
cup of calyx-like scales (four–five deep yellow crescentic
fleshy lobes alternating with narrow teeth) surrounds whole
cluster. Fruits are three-celled capsules. All the Spurges
have an acrid milky latex in canals in their stems; hence
grazing animals avoid them.

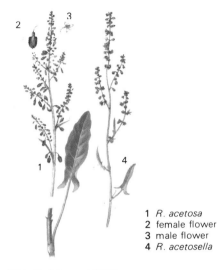

1 *R. acetosa*
2 female flower
3 male flower
4 *R. acetosella*

Fam: PGO.   *Dist:* Br Isles and W Eur.
Hab: mds, pastures. Fl 5–6.

A Dock, not to be confused with Wood-sorrel. Per herb, 30–100 cm tall; hairless shiny arrow-shaped leaves; basal leaves long-stalked, stem-leaves almost stalkless. Tubular brown stipules with fringed edges surround stem above the leaf-bases. Branched inflorescence has whorls of small reddish flowers, with the three tiny outer perianth segments typical of Docks, and three rounded inner ones without tubercles. Normally dioecious; the six-stamened male flowers are closer and less red than the females. In fruit the inner red perianth segments enlarge and surround the three-winged nuts.

Sheep's Sorrel, *R. acetosella;* ab acid pastures, sandy ar or wa; 10–30 cm tall; leaves narrower; side-lobes spread or point forward; upper leaves not clasping; silvery stipules; dioecious; bright red in 8–9.

1 flower (tubercle not
yet red)

Fam: PGO.   *Dist:* Br Isles and W Eur.
Hab: wa, field edges, hs; not mts or moors. Fl 6–10.

Upright branched per plant, 50–100 cm tall, with a stout
ridged stem; hairless, except for the undersides of the leaves
and their veins. Basal leaves long-stalked, oval-oblong, up to
25 cm long, with heart-shaped bases and blunt tips; edges
slightly undulate. Stem-leaves narrower. Inflorescence,
divided into erect branches, leafy below, bears whorls of
greenish flowers, each of which has three narrow short outer
perianth segments and three larger, erect, triangular inner
segments, 5–6 mm long; these inner segments edged with
several long teeth; one of them bears a red oval swelling or
tubercle about 2 mm long. Six stamens. Fruit, as in all
Docks, is a small triangular nut.

Curled Dock, *R. crispus*, c on wa, rds, etc, also occurs on
shingle beaches; similar, but leaves oblong, parallel-sided,
wavy-margined, narrowed to the base; inner perianth
segments all have tubercles but are not edged with long
teeth.

COMMON NETTLE   *Urtica dioica*

Fam: URT.   *Dist:* Br Isles and W Eur.
Hab: c in hbs, wds, wa, around buildings or ruins, especially on phosphate-enriched soil. Fl 6–8.

A coarse, roughly hairy per herb, 30–150 cm tall, with yellow, fleshy far-creeping rhizomes that produce erect stems in spring with pairs of opposite, oval- to heart-shaped short-stalked leaves, edged with large teeth. Whole plant above ground is closely covered with the stinging hairs; when broken, these release an irritant juice containing histamine. Inflorescences, borne in axils of upper leaves, are composed of spikes of clustered tiny green flowers with four-lobed calyces. Plant is dioecious; male flowers have four or five stamens each; females a single carpel that ripens to a one-seeded nutlet. (The unrelated harmless Dead-nettle with similar leaves, can be mistaken for Common Nettle when not in flower.)

Small Nettle, *U. urens*, smaller (10–60 cm) an plant, of similar dist, c on cultivated ground; long-stalked lower leaves; all leaves more deeply cut. Sting less severe. Each plant carries flowers of both sexes.

Fam: ERI.   *Dist:* local in Br Isles; now only in belt from central Wales and N Midlands of Eng to central Scot. Also central Ire. In W Eur locally c in Denmark, E Holland, Germany; r in France, only on uplands and mts. Fl 4–9. *Hab:* open *Sphagnum* bogs, low-lying up to altitudes of 550 m. Now much reduced by drainage of bogs.

A low shrub, usually under 25 cm tall; it is often almost prostrate. Its rhizome creeps among *Sphagnum* mosses and Cotton-sedges and produces scattered little-branched stems with smooth brown bark, which can root in the moss or peat. Leaves, 1·5–3·5 cm long, are narrowly eliptic and lance-shaped; glossy dark green above, waxy white beneath; strongly rolled-back margins. Flowers, in terminal clusters, are drooping and stalked; corolla, 5–7 mm long, globular with five out-turned teeth at the mouth, at first rose-pink, becomes almost white with age. Five tiny calyx teeth; 10 stamens; a five–celled ovary with a single style enclosed within the corolla. Fruit is a capsule producing many tiny seeds.

1 flower ×1

Fam: ERI.   *Dist:* c Br Isles, but r in Midlands; c in W Eur, but r in NW France, Belgium.
Hab: hths, moors, bogs; on hills, also low ground on poor, sandy soil; open wds or acid soils. Fl 7–9.

A bushy or straggling much-branched evergreen shrub; when old it can be 1 m tall, but is usually much shorter. Wiry stems bear close-set tiny triangular dark green leaves, 1–2 mm long; sessile, erect, in four vertical rows on the twigs, they overlap each other up the stem (not spreading out as in Cross-leaved Heath or Bell Heather). Leaves are usually hairless, sometimes grey-downy. Flowers, smaller than those of the Heaths, borne in the axils of leaves in raceme-like inflorescences along upper shoots. Each flower has a conspicuous four-lobed pale purple calyx enclosing the smaller four-lobed less conspicuous bell-shaped corolla. Eight short stamens; a four-celled ovary above corolla. Fruit is a tiny globular capsule. Flower-calyces are tough-textured and persist until the following year. White-flowered plants occur occasionally, as they do in Cross-leaved Heath and Bell Heather.

1 *E. tetralix*
2 *E. cinerea*

Fam: ERI.   *Dist:* Br Isles and W Eur; r in central Eng, N France and Belgium.
Hab: c wet or moist hths, *Sphagnum* bogs. Fl 7–9.

Small, diffusely branched, evergreen shrub up to 60 cm tall; creeping rhizomes bear many tortuous, branched, erect stems. Downy younger stems bear whorls of four narrow, grey-downy leaves, 2–4 mm long, with turned-under edges. Flowers, about 6 mm long, waxy, rose-pink, urn-shaped, spreading, in terminal umbel-like heads of 4–12 together. Four tiny sepals fringed by long, gland-tipped hairs; corolla tube, four-lobed at mouth; eight stamens encircling ovary concealed in corolla; one style. Stamens open by pores at anther tips; bear curved bristle-like processes below. Ab nectar; fruit a downy capsule.

Bell Heather, *E. cinerea*, of similar dist, but v W in Eur and on dry, not wet hths, usually among Heather. Hairless stems and leaves; glossy dark green, narrow spreading leaves, in whorls of three, are 5–7 mm long. Flowers, crimson-purple, in racemes rather longer than in Cross-leaved Heath. It has numerous short leafy side shoots.

1 berries
2 flowers

Fam: ERI. *Dist:* Br Isles, r in E Anglia; v local in W Eur. *Hab:* f in oak, beech, birch, pine wds, on acid soils; open high drier moors of W and N. Fl 4–5.

Low shrub, up to 60 cm tall, also known as Whortleberry, Blaeberry (Scot), Hurts (Surrey). Creeping rhizomes; erect branched stems, the younger green, flanged, allowing photosynthesis in mild winters after leaves shed. Alternate leaves oval, acute, tooth-edged, bright green when fresh, shedding pink bud-scales on opening. Flowers, greenish pink, urn-shaped, with five-toothed mouth, calyx in form of a ring only. Eight–ten stamens; a four- to five-celled inferior ovary. Simple style with pin-headed shaped tip. Black edible waxy-bloomed berries ripen in 7.

Cranberry, *V. oxycoccos*, f but local, a tiny prostrate shrub, creeps over *Sphagnum* in bogs; v slender stems; elliptic evergreen leaves 4–8 mm long, 1–2 mm wide. Tiny pink flowers; four turned-back corolla-lobes 5–8 mm across; red berries on long stalks. Cowberry, *V. vitis-idaea*, c in uplands of Br Isles; evergreen glossy Box-like untoothed leaves; white flowers with obvious corolla-lobes; red berries.

Fam: EMP.   *Dist:* Highlands, Islands of Scot; N Eng;
Wales; Exmoor, Dartmoor; r in S Eng and Midlands, c hilly
parts of Ire. Jutland; parts of Holland.
Hab: ab on hths, moors, mts, blanket bogs. Fl 5–6.

Easily taken for some kind of Heath, but with v different
flowers, Crowberry is an evergreen shrub with creeping
rooting stems that produce upright branches about 30 cm
tall, closely set with blunt short-stalked, alternately arranged leaves; they are oblong, untoothed, about 3–5 mm
long, dark glossy green, with margins strongly rolled back.
Tiny pinkish flowers, about 1–2 mm across, develop in the
upper leaf-axils; six tiny sepals. Plant is dioecious; three
stamens in male flowers; tiny superior ovary with several
carpels in females. Fruits, glossy black berries about 5 mm
across, technically drupes, are edible but lack flavour.

   A smaller related species, Mountain Crowberry, *E.
hermaphroditum*, occurs on higher mts; shorter, rounder
leaves; has flowers with both stamens and pistils.

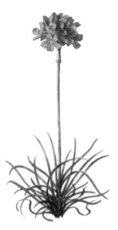

Fam: PLU.   *Dist:* Br Isles and W Eur. Fl 4–9.
Hab: c on coast, salt-marshes, sea-cliffs, shingle; also on mt ledges in N Wales, N Eng, Scot, Ire.

Neat little per herb with thick woody rootstocks from which arise dense tufts or rosettes of linear, fleshy, normally one-veined and hairless leaves, about 2–15 cm long. Flowers, fragrant, are in button-shaped heads on leafless, usually downy stems, and clasped in involucres of many chaffy brown bracts; bases of outermost bracts form a tubular sheath to the stem. Central flower of each head opens first. Each flower has chaffy five-ribbed, five-toothed tubular calyx and a pink (or white) five-lobed deeply cleft corolla about 8 mm across. Five stamens inserted on bases of petals; five separate stigmas, hairy below, arise from top of the one-celled ovary. The capsules open to release the single seed in each.

Common Sea-lavender, *Limonium vulgare*, c in salt-marshes of GB up to S Scot, and in W and N France, but absent in Ire; taller related plant; elliptical leaves; branched inflorescences; flowers purplish-blue.

Fam: PRI.   *Dist:* W Eur; Br Isles, f central Ire, r in N Scot.
Hab: locally c but decreased through cultivation in gsld on clay; still locally c on calcareous gsld and open calcareous wds. Fl 4–5.

Per herb with basal leaves, and up to 30 flowers in nodding heads on leafless scapes, 10–30 cm tall. Leaves 5–15 cm long, with winged stalks below; oval-oblong, blunt, wrinkled, downy, with shallow teeth. Deep yellow tubular corolla has five lobes forming a cup 8–10 mm across, with strong orange streaks inside. Downy calyx forms a pleated and bluntly-toothed tube around it. Five stamens on corolla-tube inside; a single pin-shaped style. Corolla 'throat' has thick folds at its mouth, as in Primrose but not Oxlip. Flowers have delicious apricot scent. In interests of conserving this lovely flower, Cowslip wine should not nowadays be made.

Fam: PRI.   *Dist:* in Br Isles only in limited areas of E Anglia; c most of W Eur, absent W France.

Hab: locally ab in moist old Oak, Ash, Hazel wds on chky Boulder Clay in parts of Suffolk, Essex, Cambs and nearby; in W Eur (where Primrose v local) is the c wd *Primula*, except on dry or acid soils. Fl 3–5.

Lovely flower, carpets its hab in spring. Per herb, rather like Cowslip, but leaves 10–20 cm long, crisply downy, longer-stalked, less wrinkled. Scapes 10–30 cm tall; calyx crisply downy, sharper toothed. Corollas clear pale yellow, 10–15 mm across lobes, which form funnel rather than cup; orange markings faint, and only in 'throat', which is open with no folds. Heads of 10–20 flowers droop to one side like a bunch of keys. Otherwise like Cowslip. Delicate peach-like scent in warm sunshine. Hybrids with Primrose (and Cowslip, r in Br Isles) occur freely where they grow close together; characters intermediate between those of parents.

Fam: PRI.   *Dist:* Br Isles (f to c, locally ab); oceanic in W
Eur, c in W France, local and coastal N France to Denmark,
Norway. Fl 3–6; rarely also 8–10.
Hab: c in wds, hbs, scrub (pastures in W) on base-rich or
heavy soils (decreasing near cities).

Per herb with whorl of v wrinkled, obovate to spoon-shaped
basal leaves, 8–15 cm long, narrowed to base, unstalked;
downy below, hairless above. Many flowers borne singly on
shaggy leafless pedicels (not scapes) 5–12 cm long, arising
from base. Flowers 20–30 mm across, v pale yellow, upright,
wheel- to saucer-shaped; corolla five-lobed; green veins and
thick folds in 'throat' of tube. Calyx-tube shaggy; five
narrow teeth 4–6 mm long. Violet-like scent in hot sun.
Plant r or absent in 'Oxlip' area of E Anglia, but where they
meet ab hybrids occur, having primrose-shaped flowers in
heads but smaller, deeper yellow, with 'throat' folds.
Primrose-Cowslip hybrid (like Oxlip, but flowers deep
yellow with 'throat' folds) is f in Eng. All Primulas have
dimorphic flowers, ie, some plants have one long, obvious,
pinhead style, and five stamens hidden in tube (pin-eyed);
others have five projecting stamens and one hidden style
(thrum-eyed); thus avoiding self-pollination.

CREEPING YELLOW LOOSESTRIFE

Lysimachia nemorum

Fam: PRI.   *Dist:* c Br Isles, except drier, more cultivated areas, ie E Midlands, Fens; NW Eur.
Hab: wds, hbs, on less acid soils. Fl 5–9.

Also known as Yellow Pimpernel, it is a creeping hairless per herb, up to 40 cm long, usually much less; tends to form mats of shoots among other herbs. Leaves v short-stalked, 2–4 cm long, oval-triangular and pointed. Flowers, yellow, wheel-shaped, 10–12 mm across; five corolla-lobes; five v narrow sepals about 5 mm long; five stamens attached to corolla opposite lobes; superior one-celled ovary. Flowers borne on slender stalks about 2–3 cm long. Fruit is a capsule opening by five teeth, unlike that of the Pimpernels (genus *Anagallis*) which opens by a lid.

  Yellow Loosestrife, *L. vulgaris*, a much taller (up to 150 cm), erect relative of fens and river banks locally in Br Isles except N Scot; has lance-shaped downy leaves up to 12 cm long, in pairs or in whorls of three; terminal panicles of yellow flowers about 15 mm across; corollas have hairless margins (whereas those of the garden escape, *L. punctata*, have gland-tipped hairs on the corolla lobes).

CHICKWEED WINTERGREEN

Trientalis europaea

Fam: PRI.   *Dist:* o in GB only north of S Yorks (one Suffolk outlier); not in Ire. In W Eur c in Denmark, diminishes southwards through Holland and Belgium; not in lowland France. Fl 5–7.

Hab: on acid shady humus; c in old Scottish Pine wds, also Oak and Birch in N Scot; Heather moors.

Charming per herb, has slender creeping rhizomes that produce delicate erect stems 5–25 cm tall, topped with whorls of five–six usually untoothed oval to lanceolate hairless leaves. From these leaf rosettes arise one or two long- and finely-stalked white flowers, 15–18 mm across, like little stars. Usually seven short calyx teeth; wheel-shaped corolla, lobed into usually seven pointed segments. Stamens reddish, opposite and equal in number to corolla-lobes; superior ovary with a single style, develops after pollination into a five-valved capsule. Plant often grows with the true Wintergreens (*Pyrola*) and the Creeping Lady's-tresses Orchid (*Goodyera repens*) in old Pine wds.

SCARLET PIMPERNEL   *Anagallis arvensis*

Fam: PRI.   *Dist:* c in Br Isles, except mountain areas; c in W Eur.

Hab: cornfields, gdns, wa; still c despite modern use of herbicides. Fl 5–8.

It is a largely prostrate hairless an herb, whose square stems also produce shortly erect branches with pairs of opposite, stalkless, oval, pointed untoothed leaves among them. Flowers, 10–14 mm across, salmon-red rather than scarlet, are borne singly on long stalks in the leaf-axils. Each wheel-shaped corolla has five spreading lobes and a short corolla-tube with five stamens attached to its base. There are five long narrow calyx teeth; ovary develops into a globular capsule about 5 mm across, which opens by splitting across transversely, forming a dome-shaped lid to release a number of seeds. Forms with blue, pink or lilac flowers occur. Scarlet Pimpernel, which is probably native on sand dunes, and prefers chalky soil, closes its flowers when rain is approaching.

Bog Pimpernel, *A. tenella*, a related tiny creeping per plant of boggy ground, generally c except in SE and central Eng, has round stems, short round leaves up to 5 mm across, on short stalks. Flowers long-stalked, bell-shaped and white, with many dark pink veins, thus appearing rosy-coloured.

AUTUMN GENTIAN *Gentianella amarella*

Fam: GEN.   *Dist:* Br Isles, except central and SW Scot, NE Ire; r in NW Eur, in France on N dunes only. Fl 8–9. *Hab:* chalk, limestone gslds; fixed calcareous dunes.

A glabrous strictly upright bi herb, normally 5–25 cm tall, with opposite pairs of stalkless oval to lance-shaped pointed leaves up the stem, which branches to terminate in small clusters of tubular dull purple or lilac flowers. Rosette of basal leaves of bluntly lance-shaped form produced in first year. Flowers, 14–22 mm long, as in all Gentians have superior ovary. Corolla-tube, greyish-yellow outside, has four–five spreading lilac-coloured lobes at apex, with a fringe of whitish hairs where they join the tube. Calyx-tube has four or five long equal narrow teeth, shorter than corolla-tube. Stamens, of same number as corolla-lobes, joined to its inside; two conjoined carpels, develop into a seed capsule.

Chiltern Gentian, *G. germanica*, a plant of chalk downs; v local in Eng from Hants to Chilterns, but the only c Gentian of N France, Belgium; broader leaves; much longer (25–35 mm) flowers, twice as long as calyx; corolla-tubes wider open, transversely-wrinkled outside.

Fam: MEN.   *Dist:* Br Isles and W Eur; r in SE and Midland Eng and in populated parts of continental Eur.
Hab: bogs, swamps, edges of lakes and tarns. Fl 5–7.

This lovely plant is a hairless per herb whose stout rhizome creeps, forming dense mats, through peaty soil and into the fringes of lakes or pools. From these rhizomes arise, above the water or peat, long-stalked trefoil leaves, with elliptical to ovate untoothed leaflets, 3·5–7 cm long; and the naked flowering stems, 12–30 cm tall, bearing racemes of white star-shaped flowers, pink-flushed outside. Each flower, about 15 mm across, has a funnel-shaped corolla, with five lobes, that bear thick fringes of white hairs like the fringe of a towel. A short five-lobed calyx; five reddish stamens; and a two-celled ovary above the corolla-tube. In fruit the globular capsule opens by two valves.

WATER FORGET-ME-NOT *Myosotis scorpioides*

Fam: BOR.   *Dist:* Br Isles and W Eur.
Hab: c on banks of streams; around ponds. Fl 5–9.

Per herb; creeping rhizomes produce stolons above ground
and erect stems 30–40 cm tall, bearing alternate oblong
lance-shaped, 3–7 cm-long, blunt leaves; stems, leaves
sprinkled with short adpressed hairs, or leaves almost
hairless. In cymes a branch each side of terminal flower;
branches produce flowers from fork outwards. They curve
like scorpion's tail; hence other name Scorpion Grass.
Flower buds, pink, open to produce sky-blue wheel-shaped
five-lobed corolla, 4–10 mm across, yellow-eyed, with short
tube. Five-toothed bell-shaped calyx covered with adpressed hairs; five stamens in corolla-tube. Four-lobed
ovary; simple style as in all Borage family; after pollination
four tiny black nuts grow in each calyx.

Wood Forget-me-not, *M. sylvatica*, similar; in wds, on
chalk or clay away from water; differs in its spreading hairs
on stems, leaves, calyces. Several smaller-flowered species,
ans of sandy ground, eg, *M. ramosissima*, with blue flowers
only 1–2 mm across.

1 one cyme of flowers

Fam: BOR. _Dist:_ Eng (especially Cotswolds and E Anglia), Wales, S Scot; r in central and N Scot; only in SE of Ire. Fl 6–9.
Hab: locally c on open downs, bare wa, on chalky or less acid sand and gravel; coastal dunes and beaches.

Attractive bi herb; in first year produces rosette of bristly, many-stalked, strap-shaped prostrate leaves, up to 15 cm long. The following June an erect stem is produced, up to 90 cm tall but usually less, rough with red-based bristly hairs, bearing alternate unstalked shorter leaves. Stem branches, bearing, above, one-sided cymes of buds like clusters of pink grapes which open to blue funnel-shaped flowers. Short calyx-tube with five narrow teeth; one short stamen inside corolla, four long purple-stalked stamens protruding. As in all Borage family, ovary within corolla-tube, four-lobed with a single central style; pollinated, it produces four rough-angled nutlets. Many insects visit the flowers.

1 *C. arvensis*
2 *C. sepium*

Fam: CON.   *Dist:* W Eur; Ire; GB, but r N, W Scot.
Hab: cornfields, gdns, wa; also near coasts in short turf, cliff tops. Fl 6–9.

A great nuisance in gdns, for its fleshy underground rhizomes quickly regenerate new plants from any fragments. They produce herbaceous creeping stems that climb over or up (always twisting counter-clockwise), any object they encounter. Leaves, 2–5 cm long, oblong to oval, arrow-shaped, are on short stalks alternating along stems. Pretty flowers, produced singly (sometimes two or three) in leaf-axils, have funnel-shaped corollas, up to 3 cm across, white or with lengthwise pink stripes; five petals so fused that lobes can be distinguished only by their folds and veins. Short five-lobed calyx; five stamens attached to bottom of corolla; two-celled ovary ripens to a capsule. Flowers have nectar and are sweet-scented.

    Hedge Bindweed, *Calystegia sepium*, plant of hs, wd borders, fens in W Eur, Ire, GB (but r northwards in Scot), much larger climbing herb; leaves up to 10 cm long; large white unscented flower-trumpets, 3–5 cm across; two large bracteoles enclosing calyx.

1 *S. dulcamara*
2 *S. nigrum*

Fam: SOL.   *Dist:* c Br Isles (not N Scot); W Eur.
Hab: hs, shingle beaches, damp wds, fens. Fl 6–9.

Member of Potato family, also called Woody Nightshade, per climber with creeping rhizome, can reach 2 m high or sprawls on ground. No hooks or twining stems; merely leans on other plants. Stalked alternate, pointed leaves, hairless or downy, and heart-shaped, oval and simple or with deep lobes or even basal stalked leaflets below. Cymes, stalked, on branches opposite leaves. Individual flowers have short five-lobed calyx; wheel-shaped purple corolla, with five lobes, each with two tiny green knobs at base and turning back in maturity. Five yellow anthers cohere into pointed cone around style; two-celled superior ovary, finally becoming oval red berry about 1 cm across.

  Black Nightshade, *S. nigrum*, c in ar or wa; smaller low-growing an plant; similar but white-petalled flowers half the size; globular black berries.

Fam: SCR.   *Dist:* f GB except N, W Scot; W Eur; o Ire.
Hab: dry banks, wa, scrub on chalk and sand. Fl 6–8.

Bi herb; in first year produces rosette of whitish-woolly
stalked oval-lanceolate leaves, up to 20 cm long; in second
adds woolly stem, 50–200 cm tall, with stalkless lanceolate
leaves whose bases run down stem. Above, a dense, usually
unbranched, spike-like raceme of yellow flowers, 1·5–3 cm
across; calyx-tube deeply lobed into five pointed teeth, and
short-tubed corolla with five nearly equal oblong lobes. Five
orange-anthered stamens, three upper with white or yellow
hairs on stalks, two lower longer and scarcely hairy. Two-
celled superior ovary; one style; fruit is a two-celled oval
capsule.
   Dark Mullein, *V. nigrum*, local on rds, downs, wa, on
chalk, sand; W Eur and S Eng; dark green, thinly downy
leaves; purple hairs on stalks of stamens.

1 single flower ×1

Fam: SCR.   *Dist:* c in W Eur, Eng, Wales, S and E Scot; r in NW Scot and Ire.
Hab: rds, hbs, field borders, wa. Fl 6–10.

This erect per herb has flowers like tiny yellow garden Snapdragons, but with long tubular spurs hanging from them. The creeping rhizomes produce upright stems 30–80 cm tall which, with their narrow strap-like grey-green leaves, are usually hairless. Stems branch to end in long racemes of yellow flowers. Each flower, 15–20 mm wide, is stalked, with narrow basal bract. Five-lobed calyx; Snapdragon-like corolla, formed of five lobes; two form the upper lip, three the lower. A bright orange swelling on the inside of the lower lip is called the palate. The spur, up to 20 mm long, yellow, hollow, pointed, containing nectar, arises from the back of the lower lip and hangs downwards. Four stamens concealed inside the corolla; a single style; superior, two-celled ovary develops into an oval capsule.

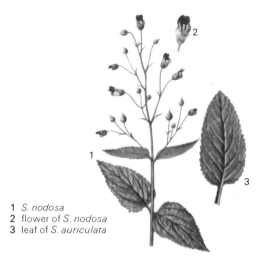

1 *S. nodosa*
2 flower of *S. nodosa*
3 leaf of *S. auriculata*

Fam: SCR.   *Dist:* W Eur; Br Isles except Shetland; r in NW Scot.
Hab: c in damp wds, hbs; not mts. Fl 6–9.

Per herb, 40–80 cm high; knotted swollen rhizomes produce erect four-angled hairless stems bearing stalked oval to heart-shaped, pointed, coarsely toothed, opposite-paired leaves 6–13 cm long. Panicle of cymes from axils of leafy bracts. Each flower stalked; short calyx-tube has five blunt chaffy-edged lobes; unpleasant smell. Corollas almost globular, about 1 cm long, have greenish tube, chocolate-coloured bi-lobed upper lip, greenish lower lip, two side lobes. Four short stamens bent down inside flower; stigma matures first, receives other plants' wasp-borne pollen, then withers; anthers then mature and liberate pollen on next wasp visitor.

Water Figwort, *S. auriculata;* similar, on river, pond banks, fens, wet wds; o on chk scrub; strongly four-winged stem; blunt leaves; white-edged sepals.

Fam: SCR. *Dist:* oceanic; Br Isles (not Shetland), r E Midlands, Fens, mid-Ire; W France, decreasing to E. *Hab:* open wds, hths, mts, on acid soils. Fl 6–9.

Downy bi herb, up to 150 cm high; produces in first year rosettes of stalked, oval to lanceolate toothed leaves (up to 20 cm long, green and downy above, grey and woolly below); in 6 of second year flowering stem (sometimes with side branches), bearing a long raceme of the familiar pinky-purple Foxglove flowers. Each flower, stalked, arises in axil of a lance-shaped bract. Calyx cup-like, deeply five-lobed; corolla-tube, 4–5 cm long, shortly five-lobed at the tip, with lowest lobe longer than rest. Inside of tube has white spots with dark purple centres. Four stamens and style inside tube. Pollination by humble-bees; stigma cannot receive pollen until pollen of own flower all shed. Fruit is an oval capsule.

   Yellow Foxglove, *D. lutea*, locally c on chk in France, Belgium, naturalized in some Eng chkpits; small yellow flowers to 2 cm long; hairless leaves.

Fam: SCR. *Dist:* W Eur; Br Isles (but r in Outer Hebrides and Shetland). Fl 4–6.
Hab: hbs, rds, open wds, old gslds; not v. acid soils.

Charming per herb with sky-blue flowers. Creeping rooting stems then ascend to produce more or less erect flowering shoots 10–20 cm tall. The stems, otherwise hairless, have two vertical lines of white hairs running up them on opposite sides; and bear pairs of opposite unstalked hairy coarsely toothed triangular leaves along them. Flowers in long-stalked racemes of up to 20 flowers each borne in leaf-axils; usually only one leaf of each pair produces a raceme. Each flower has lance-shaped bract shorter than its stalk, and a calyx of four narrow spreading lobes. Corollas, bright blue with tiny central white eye and dark blue radiating veins, are about 1 cm wide, with short tube and four broad spreading lobes. Two stamens, attached just inside corolla-tube, protrude one on each side; creamy anthers. One protruding style; fruit a flattened, heart-shaped capsule.

  Wood Speedwell, *V. montana;* f in wds in Eng, Wales (more r in Scot, Ire); similar, but smaller lilac flowers; stem hairy all round; blunt stalked leaves.

COMMON EYEBRIGHT   *Euphrasia nemorosa*

1 flower

Fam: SCR. *Dist:* Eng, Wales; less c in Scot, Ire, where replaced by other Eyebrights; France, Belgium.
Hab: c in gslds, downs, hths. Fl 6–10.

A neat little an herb, 10–20 cm tall, partially parasitic on other plants. Branched erect purplish stems are clothed with crisp whitish hairs and bear pairs of opposite, dark green, bluntly-toothed leaves along their length. Leaves usually shiny, hairless, but may have a few bristles on edges and veins below. Flowers, stalkless in upper leaf-axils, are in spike-like inflorescences. Each flower has bell-shaped veined calyx with four sharp teeth; two-lipped white or bluish corolla, 5–8 mm long, with purple radiating veins on its lips and usually a yellow spot on lower lip; upper corolla lip is two-lobed and arched forward; lower lip flat, longer, three-lobed. Four stamens below upper lip. One style; the ripe capsule is oblong, flattened, blunt, two-celled. More than 25 Eyebrights are recorded in Br Isles; *E. nemorosa* the most c in S Eng. All partially parasitic on other plants; differ in small features.

1 single flower

Fam: LAB.   *Dist:* Br Isles, except mts of Scot; W Eur.
Hab: marshes, wet mds, beside streams. Fl 7–10.

A hairy per herb with creeping rhizomes that produce square upright freely-branched stems, 30–40 cm tall. Leaves, closely hairy, stalked, oval with rounded teeth, arise in opposite pairs. Flowers quite small, lilac, aggregated into dense globose terminal heads formed of close-set whorls. Individual flowers, only about 3 mm long, have tubular four-lobed corollas with almost equal lobes; tubular, equally five-toothed calyx; four projecting stamens; superior ovary of four lobes, typical of the Labiatae, develops after pollination into four little nutlets surrounding style. Water Mint has a pleasant sharp minty smell when bruised.

Fam: LAB.   *Dist:* Br Isles and W Eur.
Hab: gslds, open wds, hbs, downs, wa, near sea; all but
wettest, shadiest, most acid places. Fl 6–9.

A creeping, sparingly downy per, with ascending or upright
square flowering stems, 5–30 cm tall, that bear pairs of
stalked oval leaves, untoothed or v feebly toothed. Flowers in
whorls in dense terminal spike-like inflorescence; each
flower in axil of a bract; bracts, much smaller than leaves,
are purple-tinged and fringed with white hairs; calyces also
purple-tinged, two-lipped, truncate at the mouth (ie, as if
cut across transversely). Upper calyx also bears three short
spines; lower, two longer ones. Calyx persists after flowering
and helps in winter recognition, as do the two leaves at base
of flower-spike. Corolla violet (rarely pink or white), two-
lipped; upper lip is much arched forward, lower convex.
Four stamens; one style. Smaller flowers without anthers
also occur. Selfheal was formerly considered of great
medicinal value.

Fam: LAB.   *Dist:* Br Isles and W Eur.
Hab: c in lowland wds, hs, shady gdns. Fl 7–9.

Per bristly herb, smells harsh when bruised; creeping rhizomes bear upright square stems, 30–80 cm tall, with pairs of opposite long-stalked pointed heart-shaped coarsely-toothed leaves. Whorls of about six flowers in bract-axils on upper stem form interrupted terminal spike 10–15 cm long. Lower bracts narrower than ordinary leaves; upper bracts lanceolate, untoothed. Calyx-tubes bell-shaped, roughly hairy, glandular, tipped with long teeth; beetroot-red two-lipped corolla, downy outside, hairless inside, has hooded upper lip, longer inflated three-lobed lower one with crimson marks on paler central patch. Four arched stamens; one style at back of flower. Anthers ripen first; stigmas then accept bee-borne pollen.

Marsh Woundwort, *S. palustris*; hab streams, swamps; lance-shaped leaves; purple-pink flowers; no smell.

Fam: LAB.   *Dist:* W Eur; c in Eng, Wales, northwards to mid-Yorks, then r; absent in Scot; only SE of Ire.
Hab: decid wds, on chalk and base-rich loam. Fl 4–6.

Yellow Archangel appears rather like a yellow-flowered and prettier Dead-nettle. It is a per herb with long leafy stolons above ground, producing 20–60 cm-tall erect square stems with pairs of acute, toothed, opposite ovate-elliptical leaves. Leaves are stalked (not with heart-shaped bases, as in Dead-nettle). Stems and leaves only sparingly hairy. Bright golden-yellow flowers in whorls in axils of upper leaves; corollas have short tubes and two long lips: the upper vault-shaped; the lower with three almost equal lobes, and spotted with red-brown flecks. Four stamens and style follow curvature of upper lip. This plant may become quite dominant during the second year after a wd has been felled or coppiced.

1 *L. purpureum*
2 *L. album*

Fam: LAB.   *Dist:* Br Isles and W Eur.
Hab: c in wa, gdns, hbs, ar. Fl 3–11.

An herb, somewhat downy, produces several square upright stems and opposite leaves. Lowest leaves v small with long stalks; leaves larger higher up and become heart-shaped, rather blunt, with large teeth, shorter stalks. Stems and leaves are often purple-flushed. Purplish-pink flowers in whorls subtended by sessile leaves on the upper stem. Corolla-tube, longer than the bell-shaped five-toothed calyx, is two-lipped, the upper lip arched over stamens and style, the lower purple-spotted, three-lobed and v convex (side lobes are v small).

White Dead-nettle, *L. album*, a much taller (to 60 cm) per plant of hbs and rds, c in Eng and S Scot; white two-lipped flowers about 2 cm long, have v arched upper lips. There is no relationship between the (hollow and square-stemmed) Dead-nettles and the (solid, round-stemmed) Stinging Nettles, merely a superficial resemblance in the hairy heart-shaped leaves.

Fam: LAB.   Dist: Br Isles (not NW Scot and some outer islands). Fl 3–5.
Hab: c decid wds, hbs, old gslds; on less acid soils.

A per herb, usually softly hairy, with creeping, rooting stems that produce more upright flowering branches. Opposite leaves, kidney-shaped to heart-shaped with netted veins and blunt teeth, have long stalks. On the erect shoots the flowers, violet- to lilac-coloured, are borne in loose whorls of three to six flowers in the leaf-axils. Each flower has tubular two-lipped calyx, and a long-tubed corolla with flat two-toothed upper lip and a hanging three-lobed, purple-spotted lower one. Four stamens; a four-celled ovary. Pink flowered forms occasionally occur, also forms with flowers twice the normal size. Ground-ivy, quite unrelated to real Ivy, is probably so-named from its habit of creeping over the ground in wds as does Ivy.

Fam: LAB. *Dist:* Br Isles, W Eur. Fl 5–7; and again often 9–10.
Hab: c in damper open wds, sheltered gslds, old mds. Not in acid mls except in base-rich flushes.

Per, sparingly hairy herb; short rhizome but long, creeping, leafy, rooting stolons and square stems, 10–30 cm tall. Root-leaves, long-stalked and tapering below, oblong, blunt above, scarcely-toothed, shiny dark green, almost hairless, form rosettes in winter. Stem-leaves, opposite paired, are stalkless and oval. Inflorescence forms a dense spike built up of whorls in axils of upper leaves. Upper bracts of spike, oval, purple-dark-blue tinted, are shorter than the flowers they subtend. Calyx, 5–6 mm long, has short teeth on its tube. Corolla a glorious blue, much of the colour in the darker veins. It has v short upper lip of two tiny teeth, and a long, three-lobed lower lip hanging down like a tongue. Four stamens and the one style arch over the flower's back below upper corolla lip.

RIBWORT PLANTAIN _Plantago lanceolata_

1 _P. lanceolata_
2 leaf of _P. major_

Fam: PLA   _Dist:_ Br Isles; W Eur.
Hab: ab disturbed, trampled ground, most gslds. Fl 5–10.

Hairless or slightly downy per herb with tap-root. Lance-shaped, long-stalked, usually untoothed basal leaves, up to 20 cm long, ribbed with strong lengthwise veins; flat in trampled places, more upright in long grass. Leafless, deeply furrowed flowering stems, up to 45 cm tall, bear cylindrical terminal spikes of tiny flowers. Each flower, about 4 mm long, has lance-shaped brown-tipped bract at its base, a green four-lobed calyx-tube, a brown-ribbed corolla-tube with four chaffy lobes, four cream-coloured long-stalked anthers and one style. Flowers, lacking scent or nectar, are unattractive to insects; wind-pollinated. Fruits are tiny two-celled capsules.

  Great Plantain, _P. major_, c in similar hab; usually hairless; smooth-stemmed; large oval leaves narrow abruptly to stalks. Hoary Plantain, _P. media_, c on calcareous gslds in Eng; oval downy leaves gradually narrow to stalks; scented, insect-pollinated flowers; white corollas, lilac-pink stamens.

NETTLE-LEAVED BELLFLOWER

Campanula trachelium

Fam: CAM. *Dist:* S half of Eng; E Wales; r in Ire; not Scot; c France, decreasing northwards in W Eur.
Hab: c open or coppiced wds, scrub, hbs; only on calcareous soils. Fl 7–9.

Per herb up to 1 m tall, with erect bristly stem bearing alternate, short-stalked bristly toothed leaves of pointed oval form (resembling that of Stinging Nettle). Basal leaves, more heart-shaped, longer-stalked, with coarser teeth. Short racemes of one–four pale purplish-blue flowers in upper leaf-axils form a leafy panicle. Short, five-lobed, calyx-tubes; corollas bell-shaped, five-lobed, 25–35 mm long, 20– 25 mm wide; five stamens attached to base of corolla-tube; one style with three stigmas; inferior ovary, as in all Bellflowers. It (not the Italian garden plant now so-called, ie, *C. medium*) is the original Canterbury Bell of Elizabethan botanists.

Clustered Bellflower, *C. glomerata*, locally c in Eng on calcareous gslds; much shorter; downy fine-toothed leaves; deep blue-purple flowers, 15–20 mm long, in dense clustered heads.

1 root-leaf

Fam: CAM.   _Dist:_ ab in GB; only local in Ire; f in W Eur.
Hab: hths, dry gslds, hill pastures, dunes, downs, rds. Fl 7–9.

Delicate per herb with creeping rhizomes; basal leaves (often withered by its flowering time) long-stalked, heart-shaped to oval, give the plant its Latin name. Hairless stems, 15–40 cm tall, bear progressively narrower leaves upwards; uppermost are linear and entire. Branched panicle of delicate drooping pale blue flowers, broadly bell-shaped with five narrow spreading calyx-teeth and five broad pointed corolla-lobes. Five stamens attached to base of corolla-tube inside; three stigmas; three-celled inferior ovary. Called Bluebell in Scotland.

Fam: RUB.   *Dist:* Br Isles except outer islands of Scot; W Eur. Fl 5–6.
Hab: c locally in wds on calcareous or base-rich soils; also in dry beechwds in S Eng.

A plant of the Bedstraw genus, it is an erect per herb, hairless except beneath the nodes; grows from far-creeping rhizomes. Square stems, pleasantly vanilla-scented when bruised, bear whorls of seven–nine smooth, cusped leaves. White flowers, in loose cymes at tips of stems only, are larger (to 6 mm across) than in Hedge Bedstraw; funnel-shaped rather than wheel-shaped; four corolla lobes. Two-celled fruits, 2–3 mm across, have hooked black-tipped bristles that cling to fur and clothes.

1 *G. mollugo*
2 *G. verum*

Fam: RUB.   *Dist:* ab in Eng, more r in Scot, Wales, Ire; c in W Eur.
Hab: hbs on clay and chk; also in chk gslds, wds. Fl 6–9.

Per herb, with stout rootstock from which arise creeping-to-erect rather weak stems, up to 1 m or more tall. Leaves, downy or hairless, in whorls of six–eight along stems, are 8–25 mm long, linear to lanceolate, usually wider above the middle. Flowers, white, up to 3 mm across, are in panicled cymes on upper parts of stems; no calyx; corolla of four pointed lobes; four stamens; two styles. Two-celled inferior ovary; the tiny two-celled fruits become black when ripe; they are wrinkled but without hooks or hairs.

Lady's Bedstraw, *G. verum*, c in much of Br Isles and W Eur, in pastures on chk or sand; narrower linear leaves, 0·5–2 mm wide, with only one vein; bright yellow flowers.

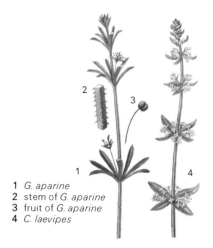

1 *G. aparine*
2 stem of *G. aparine*
3 fruit of *G. aparine*
4 *C. laevipes*

Fam: RUB.   *Dist:* ab Br Isles and W Eur.
Hab: hbs, wds, beaches, wa. Fl 6–8.

An herb with scrambling, diffusely-branched stems, up to 120 cm long, that form dense, curtain-like masses; stems, four-angled, bear tiny down-bent prickles on the angles. Leaves in whorls of six–eight, linear-lance-shaped, edged with backward-pointing prickles. Loose branched cymes of tiny greenish-white flowers, about 2 mm across; stalk of cyme bears a whorl of leaf-like bracts. Flower structure as in Hedge Bedstraw. Two-lobed fruits break into two globular purplish nutlets, covered with hooked bristles that catch on fur etc for dispersal. Plant is also called Goosegrass.

Crosswort, *Cruciata laevipes*, c in scrub, pastures, rds, especially on chk in GB (r Scot); not native in Ire; erect per herb with hairy stems; whorls of four broader, ovate hairy leaves; leaf-axils bear cymes of tiny yellow honey-scented similar flowers; but no hooked bristles.

MOSCHATEL or
TOWN HALL CLOCK

Fam: ADO.   *Dist:* GB, except NW Scot and islands; an
introduction in Ire; most of NW Eur. Fl 4–5.
Hab: f wds on base-rich loam; rock ledges up to 1200 m.

This attractive little per herb has no close relatives. It has a
creeping rhizome with fleshy scales at its apex, from which
arise slender upright unbranched stems, 5–10 cm tall. Long-
stalked basal leaves have three leaflets, each with three or
more deep lobes. Leaves, pale dull yellowish-green, have
shape of those of Wood Anemone, but more fleshy, with tiny
spines on lobe-tips; two similar, much smaller opposite
leaves on upper part of stem. At top of stem a head of five
stalkless yellow-green flowers; one faces upwards with its
parts in four; the other four face outwards like the faces of a
town hall clock, with their parts in fives. Cup-like calyx
above the inferior ovary; a four–five-lobed corolla; four (or
five) yellow stamens, each divided to the base so that their
number appears double; three–five carpels; fruit, a small
green berry-like structure, sparingly produced.

Fam: DIP.   *Dist:* Eng, Wales; more r N to Fifeshire in E
Scot; local only in Ire; c in W Eur. Fl 6–9.
Hab: f to locally c in wa, rds, pastures; by streams.

Tall bi herb sometimes mistaken for a Thistle. In first year
the stout tap-root bears a rosette of oblong prickly prostrate
leaves, about 40–50 cm across. Second year brings the stout,
branched, angled stem, up to 2 m tall; spines on angles;
opposite pairs of lance-shaped leaves, prickly only on
underside of midrib, and joined at bases to form cups in
which water collects. Flower-heads ovoid, 3–8 cm long, with
a basal whorl of upward-curving linear spiny bracts, 4–5 cm
long. Each floret in the head has a cup surrounding its calyx,
and a spiny bract much longer than itself. Calyx four-angled
and hairy; corolla, rosy-purple, has long tube and four lobes.
Stamens and the simple style protrude. Ovaries inferior in
Teasels and Scabious. The dried-out bur-like fruiting heads
remain conspicuous in winter.

Fam: DIP.   *Dist:* W Eur; lowland Br Isles; r N Scot.
Hab: c in pastures, downs, scrub, hbs, on calcareous dry soils.
Fl 6–9.

Per with strong hairy stems, 30–90 cm tall, bearing opposite-paired leaves. Root-leaves usually broadly lanceolate, undivided, short-stalked; stem-leaves stalkless with coarse segments, terminal leaf usually elliptical, laterals pinnatifid, narrow, oblong; all v hairy, dull green. Flat-topped flower-heads, 2–4 cm across, are on long stalks; each with many bluish-lilac florets on a disc-shaped receptacle; below, a whorl of bracts shorter than florets. Outer larger than central florets, have unequally-lobed corollas, with longer lobes outside; corollas of inner florets more regularly four-lobed. Calyx of eight hairy spine-like teeth; four protruding yellow-anthered stamens.

Small Scabious, *Scabiosa columbaria*, similar hab, dist; r Scot, not Ire; narrow-lobed pinnate stem-leaves; narrower root-leaves; smaller domed flower-heads; dark long calyx spines; downy, not hairy.

Fam: COM.   *Dist:* Br Isles and W Eur.
Hab: pastures, wa, rds; not high mts. Fl 6–12.

A per (sometimes bi) herb with short rootstock; erect leafy flowering stems, 30–150 cm tall, branch above the middle. Basal rosette, conspicuous in spring, of stalked, lyrate-pinnatifid leaves, 4–8 cm long, with large oval blunt terminal lobe and much narrower oblong side-lobes; all lobes toothed, normally cottony below, dark shiny green above. Stem-leaves similar, but clasping, stalkless above; lack the broad terminal lobe. Flower-heads in compact, flat-topped terminal corymbs. Each head about 15–25 mm across, with long yellow spreading ray-florets, yellow disc-florets and a bell-shaped green involucre. The flowers have structure usual in Compositae (see Introduction). The black and yellow striped caterpillars of Cinnabar Moth are c on Ragwort, often defoliating it.

Oxford Ragwort, *S. sqalidus*, c on wa in Eng since World War II; shiny hairless narrow-lobed green leaves; inflorescences looser, not gathered into umbel-like corymbs; involucral bracts black-tipped.

Fam: COM.   *Dist:* Br Isles and W Eur.
Hab: wa and ar; dunes, beaches. Fl most of the year.

A c weed, but because annual never so troublesome as pers
such as Goutweed and Bindweed. Upright branched stems,
8–50 cm tall; like the leaves, slightly hairy or hairless.
Leaves pinnatifid into rather irregularly-toothed blunt
lobes; lower leaves stalked, upper clasp stems. Tiny flower-
heads, about 4 mm across, gathered into dense terminal and
axillary clusters on the apex of stem and its branches. Each
head cylindrical, surrounded by two rows of green bracts;
outer shorter bracts have black tips. Usually no ray-florets;
tiny tubular disc-florets with structure usual in Compositae,
with five stamens in a tube and a bifid style. In fruit the tiny
achenes develop a long white pappus for wind-dispersal.

Fam: COM.   *Dist:* Br Isles and W Eur. Fl 3–4.
Hab: c on clay in ar, rds, wa, quarries, cliffs, dunes, screes.
Colonist species, pioneers new habs.

Per herb; thick white branched creeping stolons bear flower-
heads in spring, and later leaves in whose axils arise the next
year's flowering shoots. Leaves, 10–30 cm across, long-
stalked, entirely basal, roundish-heart-shaped with poly-
gonal outline and scattered teeth; white-felted on both sides
when young, on lower side only when mature. Flower-heads
borne singly on hollow scapes, 5–15 cm tall, carrying linear
blunt woolly scale-leaves. Bracts around flower-head linear,
blunt, greenish or purplish, rather hairy; before flower-head
opens the bud has appearance of shaggy pony's foot – hence
plant's name. Flower-heads, 15–35 mm across, bright yellow, with many female ray-florets and rather few tubular
male disc-florets in centre. Scapes lengthen to bear head of
nutlets each with a white pappus, the whole like a Dandelion
clock. Leaves were formerly brewed as a cough cure; also
smoked.

Fam: COM. *Dist:* c Eng, Wales, especially in S, o in Ire; very r in Scot; locally c in W Eur.
Hab: damp marshy mds, pastures, rds, open wds, ditch banks; on heavy soils. Fl 7–9.

A per herb with creeping rootstock; upright, branching stems, 20–60 cm tall, sparsely hairy, bearing wrinkled v downy oblong leaves with bases clasping stem. Bright yellow flower-heads, 1·5–3 cm across, terminate the main stems and side branches. Each consists of many closely-packed florets; the outer strap-shaped, yellow with pistils but no stamens; inner florets covering receptacle-disc are tubular, also golden-yellow, with five stamens forming a tube, and a style with two stigmas. Bracts round the heads are narrow, fine-pointed, hairy. Nutlets have a pappus of hairs which acts as a parachute in seed dispersal. Plant's specific name refers to its former use in treating dysentery.

Fam: COM.   *Dist:* Br Isles and W Eur. Fl 7–10.
Hab: coastal: c salt-marshes, tidal estuaries; o on sea-cliffs, rocks; inland salt-works Cheshire, Worcs.

Plant of same genus as garden Michaelmas Daisy (an introduction from N America). A hairless per herb; short rhizome, stout upright sparsely-branched stems, 15–100 cm tall. Alternate leaves, lance-shaped, smooth, fleshy, sometimes with a few teeth. Corymb of daisy-like heads, 8–20 mm across, and surrounded by close-set overlapping narrow blunt bracts with chaffy tips. Outer ray-florets are spreading, female only, blue-purple or, rarely, white; one variety lacks ray-florets. Tubular, bright yellow, perfumed disc-florets have five-toothed corollas and both stamens and pistil. As in all Compositae, an inferior ovary with style lobed at tip into two stigmas, but only one seed developing in fruit. Pappus hairs represent calyx (otherwise missing in Compositae); here pappus becomes brownish 'parachute' about 10 mm long.

Fam: COM.   *Dist:* Br Isles and W Eur.
Hab: ab on rds, all gslds except on v acid soil; mt rock ledges.
Fl all year; peak 4–5.

One of the best-known of our wild flowers; it is a sparsely
downy per herb, with short erect rootstock from which arise
leaf-rosettes, erect in taller grass but flat in short turf. Spoon-
shaped, sparsely hairy blunt-tipped leaves, edged with blunt
rounded teeth, narrow rather abruptly below into broad
stalks. Flowering stems hairy, unbranched, leafless, 3–15 cm
tall, each terminated by a single daisy-head, 16–25 mm
across. Each head has a conical receptacle with blunt green
bracts in one row around it, and bears outer row of white
strap-shaped ray-florets, usually pink-tipped on outside and
with inferior ovary and two-lobed style; in centre many
yellow tubular disc-florets, each with five-lobed corolla-
tube, five stamens joined into a tube, and two-lobed style.
Inferior ovaries develop into tiny achenes, but there is no
pappus. Ray-florets close inwards at night and when sun
hidden.

Fam: COM.   *Dist:* W Eur; Eng, Wales, much of Ire; less c
in Scot; not N Scot.
Hab: ab in fens, river banks, wet wds; o in downland scrub.
Not acid soils. Fl 7–10.

Per herb, 30–120 cm tall, with woody rootstock; stout
upright downy rounded reddish leafy stems, branching
above to terminate in flower-heads. Root-leaves stalked,
lance-shaped; stem-leaves scarcely-stalked, opposite, divided into three or five lance-shaped toothed leaflets up to
10 cm long; leaves on branches simple and lance-shaped; all
leaves downy and dotted with glands. Flower-heads are
dense trusses, consisting of numerous smaller heads of five–
six whitish-pink or mauve florets; each smaller head surrounded by about ten narrow purple-tipped translucent
involucral bracts. Florets, about 6 mm long, have each a
five-toothed tubular corolla, five stamens forming a tube,
and one long white style. Inferior ovary becomes a blackish
nutlet beneath a parachute-like pappus of white hairs
developed from calyx.

YARROW or MILFOIL   *Achillea millefolium*

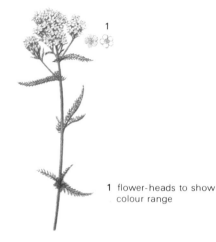

1 flower-heads to show
colour range

Fam: COM.   *Dist:* Br Isles and W Eur.
Hab: very c on rds, gslds, open spaces, grass on mts. Fl 6–10
or later.

Per, strongly scented far-creeping herb; upright, furrowed
rather woolly stems 8–50 cm tall. Basal leaves long-stalked,
upper are shorter and stalkless; all alternate and pinnately
divided two or three times into v narrow but flat and pointed
segments, giving plants feathery appearance. Flower-heads
individually small, gathered into umbel-like flat-tipped
corymbs at stem-tips, at first sight resemble those of
Umbellifers, but have usual features of Compositae. Each
head, 4–6 mm across, has (usually) five short, broad white
(sometimes pink) female ray-florets that look like an
Umbellifer's five petals; 10–12 tubular creamy disc-florets,
each with five joined stamens and a two-lobed style. No
pappus, but achenes disperse efficiently. Plant formerly
much used in medicine.

1 *M. perforata*
2 *C. suaeveolens*

Fam: COM.   *Dist:* Br Isles and W Eur.
Hab: *M. perforata* on ar or wa; per form on coastal cliffs and
beaches is now called *M. maritima*. Fl 6–10.

Scentless Mayweed, so-called to distinguish it from related
plants with a strong smell when bruised, is c in a per form
with fleshy leaves and decumbent stems, and an form with
non-fleshy leaves and erect stems. Stems, hairless, branched,
bear alternate stalkless leaves, divided several times pinnately into narrow cylindrical segments. Flower-heads, 2–
5 cm across, resemble smaller versions of the Ox-eye Daisy,
with long white female ray-florets, and numerous tubular
central disc-florets. Bracts round head form a cup and are
oblong, blunt, pale green with a narrow brown margin;
achenes have no pappus.

Pineappleweed, *Chamomilla suaeveolens*, smells of Pineapple
when crushed; related; of similar looks and dist in ar and wa;
has v conical greenish-yellow flower-heads without ray-
florets. Probably an introduction into Eur from NE Asia.

OX-EYE DAISY   *Leucanthemum vulgare*

Fam: COM.   *Dist:* Br Isles and W Eur.
Hab: c on rds, older lowland pastures, hbs, railways; prefers
less acid soils. Fl late 5–8.

Per herb with a branched woody stock and sparingly-
branched upright stems 20–60 cm tall, slightly hairy, often
hairless. Root-leaves long-stalked, oblong to spoon-shaped,
blunt and coarsely-toothed. Upper stem-leaves narrower,
stalkless, pinnately cut. Flower-heads resembling large
daisies, 2·5–5 cm across, borne singly on stem-tips. Each has
involucre of overlapping close-set green bracts with narrow
brown or purple margins below. Outer, ray-florets white, 1–
2 cm long, female, each having a two-lobed style. Each ray
tipped with five teeth, representing five fused petals. Many
bright yellow inner, disc-florets, each with a tubular five-
toothed corolla, five stamens joined in a tube and a two-
lobed style. Small achenes develop from inferior ovary.

Fam: COM. *Dist:* W Eur; Br Isles, but more r in Scot, especially in mts. Fl 7–10.
Hab: c on rds, river banks, rough lowland pastures.

A per herb; creeping stoloniferous rootstock; stiffly upright, leafy, angled stems, 30–100 cm tall; strong aromatic smell when crushed. Root-leaves up to 25 cm long, stalked, oblong in outline and pinnate, with up to 12 pairs of deeply pinnately-cut leaflets, reminiscent of fern fronds. Upper leaves stalkless, clasping, only once pinnate; all leaflets themselves deeply toothed and dark green. Open, flat-topped corymb, in which individual flower-heads yellow, 7–12 mm across; having no ray-florets but only disc-florets, they resemble yellow buttons, or daisies from which ray-florets have been removed. Each head has light-fitting involucre of leathery bracts. Disc-florets golden-yellow, tubular, with five corolla-lobes, five stamens, one style. Sometimes also marginal, female only, florets; if present these are also yellow and have hardly visible corollas. Plant may be ancient escape from gardens, for it was formerly much used in cooking and medicine.

1 single flower-head

Fam: COM.   *Dist:* W Eur; Br Isles except mts of Wales and Scot.
Hab: c on rds, hs, wa. Fl 6–9.

A rather unattractive per herb; thick branched rootstock; upright shrubby branched stems, 60–120 cm tall, reddish, grooved, angled and sparingly hairy, bearing numerous alternate leaves, deeply pinnatifid into sharp-pointed segments themselves deeply-toothed. Stem-leaves have clasping bases and are less divided above. All leaves, aromatic when bruised, have dark green, hairless upper sides; downy white undersides. Numerous ovoid flower-heads, 2–3 cm across, erect, and grouped in leafy erect branched panicles. Each head densely woolly, enclosed in oblong bracts, and contains only a few reddish-brown tubular florets. Outer florets have only pistils; inner both stamens and pistils. Unlike most Compositae, it is unattractive to insects and wind-pollinated. Achenes have no pappus.

LESSER BURDOCK   *Arctium minus*

Fam: COM.   *Dist:* Br Isles and W Eur. Fl 7–9.
Hab: c rds, hbs, wa; open wds on less acid soils.

Lesser Burdock is the commoner of our two Burdock species;
it is a stout bi herb with upright, woolly branched stems 60–
130 cm tall, sometimes more. Basal leaves have long stout
woolly hollow petioles and oval to heart-shaped leaves, grey-
cottony below, green to sparsely woolly above. Alternate
stem-leaves similar but smaller, short-stalked. Loose racemes of flower-heads on upper parts of stems; each head
dense, oval, thistle-like with purple tubular florets only (ray-
florets absent in Burdocks and Thistles). Florets all have five
stamens joined into a tube; one style, forked above; a five-
toothed corolla-tube. Involucre of numerous overlapping
bracts with stiffly spreading hooked tips surrounding each
head. Ripe achenes remain in the head, which is dispersed
intact by the bract-hooks catching on fur, etc. Later the
heads gradually break up to release achenes.
   Greater Burdock, *A. lappa*, has larger flower-heads of
globular form.

Fam: COM.   *Dist:* Br Isles and W Eur. Fl 7–10.
Hab: c in hs, pastures, downs, wa; on variety of soils.

Normally bi; long tap-root; stout erect furrowed stem,
usually v cottony above, 30–150 cm tall, bears spiny wings
or flanges vertically along it. First year's root-leaves short-
stalked, 15–30 cm long; their outline oval-lanceolate, but
each deeply pinnately cut and wavy, with two-lobed
segments and many teeth, all tipped with long stout spines.
Stem-leaves similar but stalkless and run down stem; each
has a long narrow terminal segment. All leaves prickly-hairy
above, cottony below. Flower-heads oval, 3–5 cm long, are
either solitary or in small clusters. Each head surrounded by
involucre of slightly cottony spine-tipped narrow green
bracts, outer ones bent back. Numerous reddish-purple
florets protrude as a soft-spreading bottle-brush mass; each
with five-lobed corolla, tube of five reddish-purple stamens,
one bifid style. Calyx represented by ring of bristles
developing into pappus of feathery plumes for wind dispersal
of seeds.

1 *C. arvense*
2 *C. palustre*

Fam: COM.   *Dist:* lowlands of Br Isles and W Eu
Hab: ab in rough pastures, ar, rds, wa. Fl 7–9.

A per herb with initial slender tap-root; but produces far-creeping lateral roots with many adventitious buds that form new plants (thus a v troublesome weed). Stems furrowed but unwinged, 30–90 cm tall. Basal-leaves short-stalked, oval-lance-shaped, wavy-edged, somewhat pinnatifid, with strong spines along edges and on lobe-tips. Stem-leaves similar but unstalked, clasping, more deeply cut; all leaves normally cottony below, shiny grey-green above. Flower-heads numerous, singly or in clusters on stem-tips, form loose corymbs. Each head, with involucre of green to purplish bracts, is composed entirely of dull lilac (sometimes white) tubular florets. All florets look alike; although plant usually dioecious, male heads have abortive ovaries and may even ripen a few fruits. Pappus brown and feathered.

  Marsh Thistle, *C. palustre*, very c in damp gsld, marshes and wds throughout Br Isles; tall bi herb rather like Creeping Thistle in its small flower-heads, but with continuous spine-edged wings running up stem; dark purple florets.

Fam: COM.   *Dist:* c in W Eur from central and W France to central Norway; not native in Br Isles; o naturalized in N of GB. Fl 7–9.
Hab: marshes, ditches, fens, streamsides, wet wds.

Per herb, 50–150 cm tall; erect, furrowed, unwinged stems, sparingly branched above, bear almost hairless unlobed ovate-acute, stalkless, pale green, sharply-toothed stem-leaves with clasping bases. Root-leaves stalked, oval to elliptical, either undivided or deeply pinnatifid, with tri-angular pointed lobes. Unlike those of most Thistles, leaves are scarcely spiny. Flower-heads on tips of stems and their branches; each, surrounded by oval-acute bract-like upper leaves edged with fine bristles, has cottony involucre of spine-tipped linear bracts. Pale yellow bottle-brush heads of entirely tubular florets, all with both stamens and pistils. White pappus develops into a dispersal 'parachute' on top of each achene; each main pappus-bristle is feathery with side hairs along its length.

COMMON KNAPWEED *Centaurea nigra*

1 *C. nigra*
2 *C. scabiosa*

Fam: COM.   *Dist:* W Eur; Br Isles except Shetland.
Hab: c in old mds, gslds, rds, scrub. Fl 6–9.

Per, usually roughly hairy herb, 15–60 cm tall; stout branched rootstock; v tough rigid upright stems. Leaves lanceolate, hairy, grey-green; lowest stalked and usually quite undivided. Flower-heads, 2–4 cm wide, are borne singly on ends of main stems and branches. Basal involucre of bracts, oval to globular; individual bracts have greenish stalks, mostly hidden by the closely overlapping, brown or blackish upper parts, feathered with dark bristles on each side. Florets in shaving-brush-shaped tufts, are usually red-purple and narrowly tubular; outer row sometimes larger, lacking stamens and pistils, their longer narrow spreading corolla-lobes forming crown round flower-head. Central florets have both stamens and pistils; achenes each topped by a short bristly pappus.

Greater Knapweed, *C. scabiosa*, c on chk soils in W Eur, on lime gslds in S of GB; r, local in Scot, Ire; leaves deeply pinnate, less hairy; flower-heads showier, 3–5 cm wide, all with enlarged outer neuter row.

NIPPLEWORT

Lapsana communis

Fam: COM. *Dist:* lowland Br Isles and W Eur. Fl 7–9. *Hab:* ab in wa, rds, hs, paths, open places in wds.

A sparsely hairy and upright herb, 20–90 cm tall. Basal leaves large, thin, long-stalked, lyre-shaped, with a large oval terminal lobe and usually some smaller lobes below it. Stem-leaves oval to lance-shaped, smaller, with widely-spaced marginal teeth. Stem branches freely above, terminating in v tiny flower-heads only 1·5–2 cm across. Each head has single cup-shaped whorl of eight–ten keeled narrow bracts and about eight–fifteen pale yellow strap-shaped florets. Each floret has five stamens and a bifid style. Each ovary develops into an achene 2·5–5 mm long, pale brown, devoid of pappus hairs. Flowers, opening only in sunshine, always close by mid-afternoon.

Fam: COM.   *Dist:* Br Isles and W Eur. Fl 6–9.
Hab: c in mds, dunes, rds; on all but v acid soils.

Resembles a Dandelion with taller branched flower-stalks.
Per herb with long tap-root and short stock; rosette of
roughly hairy oblong-lanceolate leaves, 7–25 cm long, with
large wavy rounded teeth; several branched flowering
stems, waxy-green, 20–60 cm tall, almost hairless, with one
or two tiny leaves, or none. Strap-shaped yellow florets in
flower-heads 2·5–4 cm across, with involucres of several
rows of narrow overlapping bracts, waxy grey-green, bristly
on their midribs. Achenes beaked on top; pappus of
feathered hairs; scales on receptacle between florets.
   Rough Hawkbit, *Leontodon hispidus*, of chk gslds; fl 6–9;
similar but smaller; unbranched v hairy stems; deeper
yellow flower-head, orange outside; achenes unbeaked, with
feathered inner pappus hairs. Autumn Hawkbit, *L: autum-
nalis*, fl 7–10 in mds, paths, r on chk; taller; branched stems
wider towards flower-heads; leaves narrow, shiny, almost
hairless. Neither Hawkbit has scales between florets.

Fam: COM.   *Dist:* f in W Eur; c in S of GB, local in Scot, dying out to N; not in mts or islands; r in Ire except on limestone.
Hab: walls; base-rich or calcareous rock; chky beechwoods. Fl 6–8.

Per herb, 25–100 cm tall; short rootstock produces lyrate-pinnatifid leaves with long-winged stalks, hairless, thin, often reddish-flushed. Stem-leaves similar but smaller, stalkless, clasp stem with their basal lobes. All leaves have a large terminal lobe, itself three-lobed. Large open panicle of tiny stalked flower-heads, held sharply erect when open, resembling a candelabrum. Each head has narrow involucre of linear bracts; usually only five pale yellow ray-florets, looking like petals of a single five-petalled flower; each floret has five stamens and a bifid style. Pappus (representing calyx) with inner row of long simple hairs, outer row of shorter ones, arises from top of beaked fruit.

SMOOTH SOW-THISTLE   *Sonchus oleraceus*

Fam: COM.   *Dist:* Br Isles and W Eur. Fl 6–9.
Hab: ab on ar and wa; dunes, shingle beaches.

Normally an herb; stout upright hollow hairless stems 20–
150 cm tall. Basal-leaves oval, stalked, edged with teeth;
stem-leaves pinnatifid with pointed and enlarged basal lobes
and broad-pointed terminal lobe; all leaves glaucous
greyish-green, hairless except when v young. Stem forms
umbellate branches above, each bearing a yellow flower-
head 2–2·5 cm across, with swollen basal involucre of
hairless narrow bracts that contracts upwards into a 'waist'
just below head. Florets all similar, strap-shaped; achenes,
rough with transverse ridges, have white pappus of unbranched hairs.
   Prickly Sow-thistle, *S. asper*, nearly as c in similar habs;
leaves spine-edged, dark glossy green, with rounded basal
lobes; flowers deeper yellow; achenes smooth. Perennial
Sow-thistle, *S. arvensis*, creeping per, 60–150 cm tall; flower-
heads 4–5 cm across, golden yellow, with densely hairy
involucres; hairs tipped with golden glands.

Fam: COM.   *Dist:* Br Isles; W Eur; much of world.
Hab: ab mds, paths, gdns, wa. Fl all summer; peak 4–5.

Per herb, varied height; stout tap-root. Basal rosette of oblong-lanceolate, almost hairless bright green leaves with large triangular serrated backward-pointing teeth. Hollow leafless almost hairless stems bear single flower at summit. Stems and leaf-stalks contain milky latex. Flower-heads have two rows green lance-shaped bracts, outer row usually turned back to form a ruff, inner erect. Florets bright yellow, up to 3 cm long, have each a five-toothed strap, five stamens in a tube, one style. Pollen unimportant, may be quite abortive; inferior ovaries normally develop into achenes without pollination (*apomixis*) as is seen if stamens excised before flower-head opens. Each achene develops a white pappus (representing calyx) for wind dispersal. Some hundreds of species exist; a few reproduce normally, rest by apomixis.

1 *C. majalis*
2 *M. bifolium*

Fam: LIL. *Dist:* c in W of Eur from N Spain to Scandinavia; widespread but local and to E in GB, as far N as Inverness; very r in SW Eng and r all but E of Wales. Not native in Ire.
Hab: dry wds, on sandy or limestone soils. Fl 5–6.

Hairless per herb; creeping rhizomes; erect shoots bearing pair oval lance-shaped pointed leaves, lower sheathing bottom part of upper; many shoots lack inflorescence. Flowering scape, 10–20 cm tall, bears raceme of deliciously-scented nodding ivory-white, stalked, round bell-shaped flowers, about 8 mm across, with bracts at their bases. Six-lobed perianth; six stamens; superior ovary of three carpels ripens into bright red globular berry.

May Lily, *Maianthemum bifolium*, very r in dry sandy wds in E Eng; c from N and central France to Scandinavia; two heart-shaped glossy stem-leaves; raceme of smaller white flowers; spreading perianth segments.

Fam: LIL. *Dist:* Br Isles, except Fens, high mts and moors, Orkney, Shetland; N, W and central France; Belgium, Holland; oceanic species, dies out to E, N.
Hab: dominant in wds on lighter acid soils; open gslds, even sea cliffs in W. Fl 4–5.

Per; bulbous rootstock formed from bases of the dark green, linear, keeled leaves (arising 2–3). Flowering scape, 20–50 cm high, hairless, leafless, bears drooping one-sided raceme of violet-blue (sometimes white) flowers. Each flower has pair of narrow bracts at its base; six identical perianth segments conjoined at base to form narrow bell-shaped tube 1·5–5 cm long, rounded below. Six cream-coloured anthers; three-celled superior ovary ripens to a three-angled capsule. Called Wild Hyacinth in Scot, where name Bluebell used for Harebell.

Fam: LIL.   *Dist:* locally c in GB, E of line from Dorset, mid-Wales, to Cumberland; in Scot up to E Ross but r and near E Coast; not Ire or Scot isles. 'Continental' species (not 'oceanic') more c in W Eur than Br Isles.
Hab: damp wds on calcareous soils. Fl 5–6.

Hairless per herb; fleshy underground creeping rhizomes bear upright naked stems, 15–40 cm tall, topped by parasol-like whorl of four (sometimes five or more) leaves, 6–12 cm long, net-veined, obovate, acute, with wedge-shaped almost unstalked bases. From centre of whorl, on stalk 2–8 cm long, arises a single upward-facing flower, with four (sometimes five or six) lance-shaped green sepals 2·5–3·5 cm long, and equal number of narrower green petals. Above these a whorl of long narrow stamens, equal in number to petals and sepals together; superior purplish ovary with four or five cells; each cell has long purple stigma. Fruit black, globular, fleshy; but splits as capsule.

Fam: AMA.   *Dist:* Br Isles, but r in Scots mts and in Ire; not Orkney, Shetland. C in W Eur. Fl 4– early 6.
Hab: c moist wds, on chky or clayey base-rich soils.

Per herb, narrow white bulb produces two or three green oval-elliptic leaves, 10–25 cm long, 4–7 cm wide, with pointed tips and long stalks twisted through 180°. Flower-heads of six to twenty white star-like flowers are in dense flat-topped umbels on summit of naked, usually three-edged scapes, and spring from papery two-lobed spathe. Each flower, 16–20 mm across, has six equal perianth segments, separate down to their base; six stamens; a three-celled superior ovary. All parts of plant have characteristic garlic or onion smell, v evident when it is trampled on. The Garlics and Onions were formerly put in the Lily family because of their superior ovaries; most botanists now prefer to put them in the Amaryllidaceae because of their umbel-like in-florescence with a spathe.

Fam: AMA.   *Dist:* Eng, especially SW and Welsh borders;
E Wales; only naturalized in Scot and Ire. W of W Eur to
Belgium and the Rhine.
Hab: v local in wds and old pastures. Fl 3–4.

From Onion-shaped underground bulb arise a few glaucous
grey-green linear leaves, 12–35 cm long, slightly channelled
on inner sides. Flowers, much smaller than those of most
cultivated Daffodils, only 35–60 mm wide, are borne single
on naked, slightly flattened, leafless scapes; papery pale
brown spathes enclose flower-bases. Perianth of six equal,
pale primrose yellow floral leaves is superior to green three-
celled ovary. From perianth centre arises corona, a tubular
golden yellow structure, 15–22 mm long, slightly wider at its
many-toothed mouth; six stamens attached within; long
style with three-lobed stigma. Ovary ripens into three-celled
globular capsule. Pollination mostly by humble-bees. In
most cultivated Ds corona same colour as perianth.

YELLOW IRIS
Iris pseudacorus

Fam: IRI.   *Dist:* Br Isles and W Eur. Fl 5–7.
Hab: c ditches, fens, wet mds; by rivers, lakes.

Fleshy creeping per rhizome; erect leaves strongly keeled,
folded inwards on either side, are all in one flat plane. Erect
stems, 40–150 cm tall, rounded, are simple or branched; at
their summits flowers in groups of two or three, arising from
within two elliptical leaf-like sheathing papery-edged
spathes. Each flower bright yellow, 8–10 cm across, has
three broad oval outer perianth segments, outspread and
pendent at tips, usually purple-veined with orange spot near
base; and three much narrower, shorter, spoon-shaped erect
inner segments. All six segments joined in a tube below,
arising from top of three-celled ovary. Three stamens all
arch outwards above outer perianth segments; above each
stamen one arching style (resembling a petal). Stigmas on
style-tips, but protected by flaps from self-pollination by
anthers of own flower.

1 *L. ovata*
2 *P. chlorantha*

Fam: ORC.   *Dist:* Br Isles and W Eur. Fl 5–6.
Hab: wds, gslds; fc on base-rich chk or clay.

Creeping rhizomes; stout stems, 30–60 cm tall, bear, 5–
10 cm above ground, a single pair of opposite, egg-shaped,
blunt, ribbed, unstalked leaves, 5–10 cm long. Above them
downy stem bears one or two tiny bracts and then the
elongated cylindrical inflorescence of greenish flowers. Each
flower has green ovary; hood of three green sepals, two
petals; yellow-green lip divided half-way into two strap-
shaped parallel segments that hang down vertically; no
spur; central furrow of lip secretes nectar. By pressure on lip
tiny insects trigger off explosive device shooting pollen onto
their heads.
  Greater Butterfly-orchid, *Platanthera chlorantha;* fc in wds,
mds on basic soils; one pair opposite leaves, elliptic, lanceolate, up to 15 cm long, 3–5 cm wide; larger greenish-white
sweet-scented flowers; narrow long-spurred undivided lip;
long narrow sepals.

1 *G. conopsea*
2 *A. pyramidalis*

Fam: ORC.   *Dist:* Br Isles and W Eur. Fl 6–7.
Hab: locally c; typical form on chk, limestone gslds of Eng; larger in fens; smaller in hill pastures in N and W of GB (perhaps three separate species).

Digitate root-tubers; narrow, glossy green unspotted strongly-keeled leaves arise not in rosette but in two vertical ranks at stem-base; similar leaves up stem, which is 20–45 cm tall. Dense cylindrical spike of many flowers, each lilac-pink, strongly fragrant; spreading strap-shaped sepals; upper petals form tiny hood. Lip shortly three-lobed, unspotted, normally about as broad as long (wider in fen plants, narrower in N ones); slender spur is twice as long as inferior ovary, which forms a 'stalk' to the flower.

    Pyramidal Orchid, *Anacamptis pyramidalis;* on chk gslds, sand-dunes; c locally in Eng, Ire (r Scot); W Eur; fl 6–8; leaves grey-green, spirally borne; inflorescence carmine-purple, shorter, dome-shaped; lips broader, side-lobes longer, spreading; spurs rarely longer than ovary; 'foxy' scent.

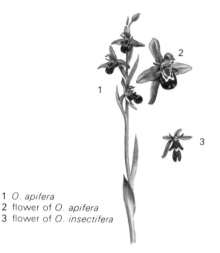

1 *O. apifera*
2 flower of *O. apifera*
3 flower of *O. insectifera*

Fam: ORC.   *Dist:* Eng, Wales; r in Ire; not Scot; c in N
France, dies out NE to Holland, Fl 6.
Hab: locally c some years on chk, limestone gslds.

Two globose tubers produce: in autumn rosette of elliptical-
oblong pointed grey-green parallel-veined leaves; and in
June stem 15–45 cm high, bearing some smaller leaves and
two–eight or more large, widely-spaced flowers, each with
large bract. Three pointed sepals, pink with greenish central
vein; two downy upper petals, shorter, square-ended,
usually green. Long furry convex lip, resembling humble-
bee on pink flower, is dark brown; has, above, U-shaped
yellow loop enclosing orangish patch; also two eye-like
knobs; long tooth curled under tip; two side lobes. No spur,
no nectar; eventual self-pollination.
    Fly Orchid, *O. insectifera*, f in chky wds, downs, in Eng,
Wales, and in Irish fens; smaller flowers, with green sepals;
narrow purple-black petals; red-brown lip shaped like a fly
with folded wings and blue patch on its back.

Fam: ORC.   *Dist:* Br Isles and W Eur. Fl 4– early 6.
Hab: locally f in base-rich wds; mds, chky gslds.

Two ovoid tubers produce basal rosette of unstalked, oblong
parallel-veined, glossy green, purple-blotched pointed
leaves. Stem, 15–60 cm tall, bears a few leaves and spike of
10–30 purplish-red flowers, each with narrow purple bract,
purplish-grey ovary, three sepals, three petals. Side sepals
spread backwards; upper one connives with the two upper
petals to form a hood; lower petal forms tri-lobed, spurred,
crimson-dotted lip, 8–12 mm long. At back of flower one
unstalked anther holds two pollen masses on stalks that
adhere to heads of visiting insects for cross-pollination;
below anther stigma surface receives pollen brought from
other flowers. Tom-cat smell.
    Green-veined Orchid, *O. morio*, in open mds in Eng,
Wales, mid-Ire; fl 5; similar, shorter; unspotted leaves;
close hood of green and purple-veined sepals.

COMMON SPOTTED-ORCHID

Dactylorhiza fuchsii

1 one flower ×1

Fam: ORC.   *Dist:* W Eur, Br Isles; not N Scot. Fl 6–7.
Hab: f wds, mds, downs; on chk, base-rich loam, clay.

Digitate root-tubers; basal rosette grey-green leaves with
transversely-placed purple spots (those of Early Purple
Orchid are darker and placed lengthwise); solid leafy stem,
15–60 cm high, bears dense cylindrical spike of pink (or
white) flowers; all petals and sepals marked with purple-red
lines. Sepals spread; the two upper petals form hood; lip,
10–15 mm wide, is three-lobed, middle lobe longest. Anther,
stigma much as in Early Purple Orchid; on back of lip a
cylindrical-conical spur, 5–8 mm long.

Heath Spotted-orchid, *D. maculata*, similar; moist acid
peaty soils on hths, bogs, moors, in Br Isles and NW Eur, most
c on uplands; leaves more pointed, with rounder spots; broad
triangular lip, only shallowly divided into three teeth, middle
one small, shorter than laterals.

178

1 fruiting head

Fam: ARC.   *Dist:* Br Isles except N Scot; W Eur northwards to S Sweden.
Hab: c wds, hs. Fl 4–5.

Deep massive tuber bears long-stalked, arrow-shaped netveined (not parallel-veined as in Lilies and Irises) glossy green leaves often purple-spotted. Stout fleshy stem, topped by large yellow-green spathe which unrolls to resemble monk's cowl, open one side; height then 20–30 cm. Inside is spadix, purplish column bearing flowers below in cup of spathe-base (not visible unless dissected); spathe waisted above cup, where ring of bristles (sterile flowers) closes it off. Below bristles a dense ring of red-brown anthers; below these ring of one-celled ovaries. Small flies pushing inside may pollinate stigmas; bristles wither to allow their escape upwards only when stamens ripe and insects can carry away plant's pollen to another plant. Also called Cuckoo-pint, Jack-in-the-pulpit, Wild Arum.

Fam: TYP.   *Dist:* W Eur; Br Isles except N, W Scot.
Hab: c in lakes, ponds, swamps, riversides. Fl 6–8.

Robust upright per with creeping rootstocks; erect, hairless
stems, 1·5–2·5 m tall. Leaves grey-green, parallel-veined,
10–20 mm wide, linear, are taller than inflorescence; their
bases sheath stem. Cylindrical inflorescence, 20–30 cm long,
top stem. Lower, brown part comprises female flowers,
densely packed together with slender brown hairs and
scales; upper, tapering, yellow part composed of male
flowers. Each female flower has a one-celled stalked ovary;
each male flower two–five stamens joined into a tube. Wind
dispersal of seeds, capsules using tufts of hairs as 'para-
chutes', occurs in 2 of following year. Often wrongly called
Bulrush (correct name for *Scirpus lacustris*, a Sedge).

INDEX

186

CHECKLIST OF SPECIES SEEN

Both families and species arranged alphabetically

Species	Place	Date

Adoxaceae – *Moschatel Family*
Moschatel or Town Hall Clock . . . .

Amaryllidaceae – *Daffodil Family*
Daffodil, Wild . . . .
Ramsons . . . .

Aquifoliaceae – *Holly Family*
Holly . . . .

Araceae – *Arum Family*
Lords and ladies or Wild Arum;
   Cuckoo-pint or Jack-in-the-pulpit . . . .

Araliaceae *Ivy Family*
Ivy . . . .

Boraginaceae – *Borage Family*
Forget-me-not, Early . . . .
Forget-me-not, Water . . . .
Forget-me-not, Wood . . . .
Viper's-bugloss . . . .

Campanulaceae – *Bellflower Family*
Bellflower, Clustered . . . .
Bellflower, Nettle-leaved . . . .
Harebell or Bluebell (Scotland) . . . .

Caryophyllaceae – *Pink Family*
Campion, Bladder . . . .
Campion, Red . . . .
Campion, Sea . . . .
Campion, White . . . .
Chickweed, Common . . . .
Mouse-ear Chickweed, Common . . . .
Pearlwort, Procumbent . . . .
Ragged-Robin . . . .
Stitchwort, Greater . . . .
Stitchwort, Lesser . . . .

Chenopodiaceae – *Goosefoot Family*
Glasswort, Annual . . . .
Glasswort, Perennial . . . .

Cistaceae – *Rockrose Family*
Rockrose, Common . . . .

Compositae – *Daisy Family*
Aster, Sea . . . .
Burdock, Greater . . . .
Burdock, Lesser . . . .
Cat's-ear . . . .
Colt's-foot . . . .
Daisy, Common . . . .
Daisy, Ox-eye . . . .
Dandelion . . . .

188